Just Words 2

...More than Words

www.justmikethepoet.com

Editor's Remarks

He's done it again! Your favorite, beloved urban poet and rhythmical genius, with a knack for his clever play on words, Michael E. Reid, is back with *More Than Words*! A highly anticipated compilation of poems with messages to speak to your mind, heart, and soul—he is opening up and lending an ear and a word to support you in the work you need to do to better yourself and the world around you, starting with your role and the affect you have in the lives of those around you!

In *Just Words,* you let him tell you all about himself in hopes that the lessons he's learned the hard way and experiences that made him better might benefit and grow you mentally, spiritually and emotionally, and now he has words for YOU! Having bared all in his first book, Mike has written *Just Words 2* as a platform to address a spectrum of issues penetrating the lives and minds of many of us within mainstream society, bringing awareness and accountability to the forefront in hopes of inspiring change yet again. So if you started with him then, realize where you are now and know that it may not be the beginning, but there's still work to be done and progress to be made—in your relationships, your neighborhoods, your families and in YOU, and the only way you can address it is by working on everything one thing at a time. In *Just Words 2: More than Words,*

Mike is here as a listener and a guide to equip you with the tools and advice you need to make the necessary changes—all you need to do is turn the page and receive the message—one word at a time.

In this world, we all need somebody—to listen, to offer advice, to commend us when we're on the right path and to redirect us when we seem to have gotten a little off track. It's understandable to make mistakes, especially when you don't know any better, but when you know better, you do better. Let "Just Words" be that guide for you, to make you better and to help you show and improve.

Meloni C. Williams

Public Service Announcement

"Before we continue, let's get a few things out of the way"

Newsflash!

I am not perfect!

I've been to Planned Parenthood more times than I will ever be a father.

I've got some tough questions for my own mother and father, but ask — to be honest, I probably won't ever bother.

I was a follower for a large portion of my life,

before I started doing this "leader" thing.

My family life was far from perfect.

My father left. My mother wasn't always right. I lost an uncle to the repercussions that using heroin needles bring.

I've worked at McDonald's.

Not all of the women I've dated were video vixens and models.

My biggest fear is to die a bachelor, without once changing a daughter's pamper or feeding a son a bottle. I wasn't always comfortable with who I was, so I tried being somebody else.

When that didn't work, I became another colored boy who contemplated suicide.

I didn't want to die though.

I just wanted somebody to see that I needed help.

I've never hit a woman or cheated on one, but there are a few that I have hurt with words, attitudes, and actions.

I've smoked, drank, might have OCD, and have claimed other people's children on my taxes.

So no I don't think I'm famous; yeah I'm "@justmike_" but I'm just like you.

And of course they were never "just words," and that's why I'm nervous about "Just Words 2."

I make my own life miserable to keep other people happy.

I too have been guilty of being superficial.

I didn't do air headed, or nappy.

I could've slept with a lot more women if I wanted to, but I respected them, sometimes more than they respected themselves.

Sometimes the ones that are always helping others could use some of the help themselves.

So I started taking my own advice.

By the grace of God I'm at a better place in my life,

even though things are still far from perfect.

The trick is to count your blessings and not your problems.

Strive for greatness. Settle for worth it.

Contrary to popular belief, no I'm not a "ladies' man."

I don't write poetry to use it as an opportunity to impress the ladies.

Man, oh man.

I'm just a man that wants women to know that it's okay to be a lady.

Damn.

If more men did what their grandfathers did, a lot of the stuff I say would be pretty useless.

But they don't.

The new girl gets taken to Ruth Chris,

But when the mother of their children calls asking for half of the daycare cost, all she gets are excuses.

If more women had the same passion for independence as they do for Nordstrom, Neiman's, and Sak's

They'd get their check for all the work they put in the office, not the bedroom.

Do you get direct deposit?

Or is the only time you get invested or deposited in; is when you're lying on your back?

Am I wrong for wanting to change the world?

I sure as hell hope I'm not.

I'm just trying to do my part.

I'm trying to rescue those hanging themselves from the tree of life;

I'm just praying that the rope won't pop.

I'm praying that the hope won't stop.

I'm just praying that you use these words the moment you receive them, because it's never too late for a new beginning.

It's also never too late for you to drop out of a race if you can't see yourself crossing the finish line and winning.

Dear Reader,

Thank you. Thank you for your purchase of "Just Words 2". With this purchase comes a challenge; a challenge to take a long hard look at your life. A challenge to ask yourself some tough questions, and possibly make some difficult decisions about where you are, where you want to be, how you are going to get there, and who you allow to go with you on your journey.

Too often we as a people settle. Settle with our career, settle with our relationship, and settle with our selves. From this day forward, settling is no longer an option. You must do better. You must want to do better. First you must realize that the way you are doing things now may not be in your best interest.

Use these words as a guide to navigate you through life's obstacle. Remember, footprints on the moon are proof that anything on Earth is possible.

May these words ignite fire inside of you that will change your life forever.

Respectfully,

Michael E. Reid

More than Words

"To truly be free, you must first break away from those things that are holding you hostage."

There's light at the end of the tunnel.

Keep hope alive. You're going to make it out of this jungle.

Rumble child. Rumble.

Use these words as a weapon. Use these words as protection.

Use these words when you may not have any words of your own.

Keep pushing forward; because at the end of the day it's really the only direction.

These are words for the world, but our conversations may never leave home.

These are words to help you realize that sometimes "real" is just a disguise.

These may be the words to convince you that you just might be better off being alone.

Some of these words may cause tears to be shed, hearts to feel heavy, remove levees, while others might make toes curl.

These are words for the weak, words for the streets, words written to create a race of tough guys and strong girls.

Don't let what was put here to shape you ultimately break you.

You're only as strong as you believe.

True strength comes from being battle tested.

Failure is not an option. You may only achieve.

These are "Just Words," a conversation between friends.

Some words may take your level of existence to new beginnings.

Other words may strike a nerve,

because they might be what you were thinking but never heard, and be exactly what you needed, the means to an end.

While these are my words, the choice is yours what you do with them.

When life's lessons have you stressing and you are brought to your knees, you're in the perfect position to pray about it.

Never ever let anyone take your joy; if they don't appreciate your existence, give the two of you some distance.

When people bring these things upon themselves, who cares if they feel some type of way about it.

I want you to know that I'm here for you,

to shed a tear for you,

to be the missing piece when the ones you once loved
said peace—when they were the ones who were
supposed to be standing right there with you.

I want you to know I care for you.

I'm going to need your help though.

Let these words stick to you like Velcro.

Let these words change the way you think a little.
Some might even help you grow up though.

Or realize that sometimes growing up has some pretty
grown responsibilities.

This may require me to be the big brother, best friend,
or father you never had.

Even though I may make a fuss,

it's only to let you know that some of the decisions
you're making are destroying us.

Glutton for Punishment

"A man who isn't willing to fight for you isn't a man worth having."

She hates men.

I'm not the reason though.

I'm just her new favorite punching bag.

because life's punches have battered and bruised her.

From an abusive ex-boyfriend, a mother who wasn't quite ready to raise a queen yet, and a sorry excuse for a dad.

So I understand where the anger was born,

but now that she has the strength to fight back, I'm the one who gets hit with the jabs.

Jab: "The less I tell him, the less he can hurt me, so I'm just going to play it cool, and if things get difficult I'm going to run first,

so he won't be the next man to desert me."

Jab: "I'm going to keep my options open and talk to other men outside of him."

Jab: "All men are liars anyway, so it's okay if I can't prove he has lied already, he's going to eventually, so, no I won't feel bad if I have to lie to him."

Jab: "I'll tell him I love him, when I don't."

Jab: "I won't tell him I love him, when I do."

Jab: "I won't tell him I'm pregnant,

I'll just make the appointment and get the abortion, because I can't raise a child on my own. He was going to be a deadbeat like my dad anyway, so who cares about what he wants to do."

Jab: "I'll make myself not trust him."

Jab: "I'll tell him how much I hate my ex-boyfriend, but behind his back I'll still fuck him."

Jab: "I'll keep asking him the same questions over and over. They all slip eventually, so I'm going to wait for the day I can bust him."

Humph...and they say love doesn't hurt.

They must have never dated a woman after she's been cheated on or beat on.

They must have never been a Mr. Rebound to a woman after her last boyfriend didn't put her on a pedestal,

instead he just used her as a doormat for him to wipe his feet on.

But will I leave?

Nope.

I'll go harder in fact, because now I realize that she needs me more.

I want to give her the type of love they make movies about.

The type of love she's never seen before.

So keep the Jabs coming baby girl because I'm a glutton for punishment.

I'm going to use every bone in my body that she hasn't broken to love her regardless.

If all the men that came before me were bullshit, it's okay; my response is, "Sweetheart, I'll be the toilet."

I'll tell her to meet me in the bathroom.

So I can flush her insecurities.

Maybe then she'll love me.

Spring Cleaning

"Don't expect the people around you to change; change the people that you keep around you."

When Spring has sprung.

I'm going to need for you to clean out more than your basement, back room and closet.

What about your bedroom?

What about your bank account?

Stop allowing people to withdraw from your life if they're not around when you need a deposit.

You keep a bunch of friends around because you think there's always strength in numbers, and you assume that by adding more people you add power to your circle.

What you've got to realize is, the more you let your guard down and welcome new people into your circle,

Now that's more people that possess ways to capitalize on your weaknesses and subsequently have the power now to hurt you.

It's time to take the power back.

Clean out your head, heart, phone book,

and the open door policy you have with who you let in your sheets.

If they only come to you with their hand out, stick your hand out too, then put two fingers up and tell them peace.

From this day forward, you don't owe anybody a damn thing.

But in the same breath, don’t get disappointed when people let you down, because nobody owes you anything either.

If people think they have the right to treat you any kind of way because of their position in your life,

have a good laugh about that.

Then treat them like a stranger from then on, and eventually you’ll make them a believer.

You came into this world by yourself and will be leaving the same way.

So, the moment someone takes your kindness for weakness be done with them the same day.

People can only let you down once; the second time is always your fault, you can only be nice to nice people.

Before you open your mouth and tell anyone you want them, first let them prove to you that they need you.

Don't ever let anyone take your joy.

Especially when they didn't give it to you in the first place.

Kill them with kindness.

A smile is the best defense against an enemy's worst face.

If they try to bring you down see it as a compliment, it only means you're above them, so love them.

Because when you fight fire with fire you might end up getting burned.

Before you give you heart, soul, time, or anything else you can't replace, make sure it has the capability of being returned.

"I know I'm not perfect. That's why I don't look for perfect. I look for real. I'm looking for somebody who is just as confused about life as I am, and hopefully we can figure it out together. I'm looking for somebody who's been hurt before because I've been hurt before. Hopefully, together we can heal each other. I'm looking for somebody who still believes in love—"old love," "we're in this together love." I want to prove to them that it still exists, so they can prove to me I'm not a fool for still believing."

-Mike the Poet

Let's Go!

"If your dreams don't scare you, they aren't big enough"

If you woke up this morning and you're not where you want to be in life; that is perfectly ok. Don't beat yourself up about that. But if you don't have a plan yet on how you're going to get there, then you have some work to do.

A life without a purpose is just an existence.

What are you waiting for? Opportunity only dances with those who are already on the dance floor.

Who are you waiting for? Anyone who isn't holding you down is holding you up.

What are you scared of? Failure is nothing more than an opportunity to try again.

Who are you scared of? Your only competition is the person you were yesterday.

Why are you waiting? Nothing comes to a sleeper but a dream.

Who is going to stop you? There are only 2 people on Earth that can stop you from doing anything you can put your mind to: that's you, and whoever you let.

This is your life. To be lived how you see fit.

They can take your possessions.

Never let them take your dreams

Bitch Please

"If you don't treat yourself like a queen, no one else will."

Excuse my French but,

A lot of these "bitches" have the "game" fucked up.

And before you interrupt,

The only reason I call them "bitches," is because I don't want to get their nicknames fucked up.

"Pretty mixed bitch."

"Filthy rich bitch."

Breaking News: You will never truly discover yourself as long as you refer to yourself as "his bitch."

"Fly bitch."

"Ride or die bitch."

When I think about what you're doing to yourself I just want to cry bitch.

I'm not sure about the type of men you deal with but,

You can pack your things the same day you EVER hear me refer to you as, "my bitch."

Everybody wants to be "his little cool ass bitch from the west side."

That's until he has sex with you, washes himself off, and then goes home to hop in bed with his wife.

He sleeps on the left side.

You didn't know that did you?

That's because he's doesn't sleep at your house.

He just creeps at your house.

You cook him dinner and feed him you for dessert.

You make me want to build a diner inside of a whorehouse.

Sweetheart, the man for you is a senior at Morehouse.

Or at least he spends less time in the streets,

and he doesn't always want you naked and under the sheets while he's at your house.

His only dream is to be your spouse.

He'll open your car door for you,

instead of closing the car door, opening his zipper and telling you to open your mouth.

Ouch.

I think you need to open your mind though.

Before you look up and you're 30 and are asking yourself, "Where the hell did the time go?"

Explain the logic in this to me;

You go out of your way to make sure you bring your scarf, so you don't mess up your 30-inch weave.

But not once do you even contemplate bringing a condom to protect what's 18 inches above your knees.

Please!

Remind yourself that no matter what adjective you put in front of it, the word "bitch" can never be seen as a compliment.

That is a fact that requires no extra thought, just a little "woman's intuition" self-respect, and some common sense.

So if he says "as long as his bitches love him" and there's a possibility he could be referring to you as one of them,

be the woman you were prior to the invention of "bad bitches", "real bitches", and the rest of them, pack your things and be done with him.

Questions

"Capable and Ready are two different things"

I know you two love each other, but are you sure you're ready? Not to spend the night together. Not to take a trip together. Not to move in together.

To create a life together.

I know he calls you his baby, but are you really ready to give him one? I know you like being inside her, but are you ready to handle the responsibilities of what will be *pushed* out, if one night you don't *pull* out? I know you like spending time together, but how about every day, all day, no days off; no "I think we should take a break"

Are you sure you're ready?

Are you sure you're ready to trade your taste for high end restaurants because they don't have a kids menu and high chairs? Are you ready to trade vacations in Las Vegas and Miami for Lego Land and Disney World? Are you ready to trade sleeping in for sleepless nights? Are you ready to trade happy hour for football practice, ballet class, PTA meetings, bakes sales, school plays, after school programs, homework and family time? Are you ready to trade Cinemax for Nickelodeon, Law and Order for Sponge Bob? Going to the moves at 12am for going to the movies at 12pm Are you ready to trade in the coupe for a Minivan?

How about this conversation at 3am on a Monday: "Wake up it's your turn." "But I changed him last." "But I have to get up for work before you." "But I carried him for 9 months." "But I had to live with you for 9 months while you carried him." "But I'm tired." But I'm not?" Now you're both up, and angry.

Where is all of this going to happen?

Does your job have benefits? Does your apartment have 2 bedrooms? Who's going to move in with whom? How far is that from your job? How good is the school district in your neighborhood? Who are your neighbors?

What about you two? Are you two strong enough?

Have you known each other long enough? Have you created enough memories as a couple before creating memories as a family? Have you laughed together? Have you cried together? Have you traveled together? Have you done everything you said you wanted to before your life changed forever? Can you look that person in the face, and then think to yourself, you know what, "I wouldn't want to be with anyone else for the rest of my life." Or at least until the child turns 18 and says, "Mom, Dad, you don't have to pretend anymore."

What about the other 197,311 questions I didn't ask you? If you're still not sure. Then ask yourself this one question.

Are you ready to be 100% responsible, accountable, and aware, of the entire existence of another human being, from feeding, changing, washing, clothing, carrying, and protecting? Every day. All day. For the rest of your life? Now some people are going to say,

"Well who is?" and my answer to them is... a Condom.

Crystal

"Sometimes, it's not about who you want, it's about who wants you"

Everybody isn't "decent" to everybody.

That's why you've got to pay attention to those people who pay you attention.

Your ghost isn't felt in every hallway.

There are some changes that need to be made in your love life, and it's my recommendation that you start today.

With rule number one being: Like Who Likes You.

If you give your time, energy and potential for memories to people who get the picture, trust me, you will not lose.

The problems appear when you go left, and start settling for random texts and pretty good sex. It is then that you begin to die a slow death.

The crazy part is, you already know what pain feels like. So I'm asking you: Why get stabbed again?

You can't create a future with someone who had an opportunity and couldn't win you; there is no future in investing in a has-been.

Your feelings get smoked like grass to them.

There is a position for everyone that you have ever let cross your path. The proper place is the past for them.

You have others around you that worship the ground that surrounds you.

Yet you put on makeup, fix your hair and nails for the only one out of the bunch that clowns you.

I bet they're happy as hell they found you.

If you put half as much effort into moving on as you do into making it work,

you'll realize that the only work that's done in a real relationship is outdoing each other's love, not healing the hurt.

While you give them everything they want, they give you absolutely nothing in return.

The song says, "Let it burn" for reason, but you're just going to keep getting burnt instead, huh?

The fact that you hate sleeping alone allows you to bring just anybody in your bed, huh? Get the fuck out of here!

What you tolerate is what you will receive. Not a penny more.

So your first priority should be being strong enough to not allow yourself to be treated like an option anymore.

Dear Mike, There's this person I've been seeing and I don't know why but I can't let them go. They cheated on me once before but I took them back because they said it was an accident. They said they were sorry, and that they want me to stay. I know they say forgive and forget, but I'm just so hurt, and I'm so lost, what should I do?

Stay? Really? For what?

So they can do it again?

Then, say sorry again?

Let me guess, and then they'll promise to do better again, right?

If I were you, my response to them would be "Thanks, but no thanks." They should only get one shot with you. That's all a person really needs. It's not your fault they had their shot and messed that up. They just thought you were going to be like the rest of them and take them back.

*I know people always say forgive and forget. I think people really misunderstand what it means to forgive and forget. My 'forgive and forget' works a little differently. So should yours. I will **forgive** myself for wasting my time with someone who didn't have their shit together. Then, I will **forget** they ever existed. Good Luck.*

-Mike the Poet

Keep Your Head Up

"The only thing you should feed ignorance with is silence."

Hey Asshole!

I bet you didn't know the girl that wears that lace front wig has cancer.

Or the girl that "walks funny: ran away from Juilliard and her dream of becoming a dancer.

Why? Because we made her.

How? Because we passed judgment based on appearance, opened that big mouth of our and "played" her.

That's the problem with us "cool" people

We look at people funny if they don't look how we do.

You laugh at the girl who wears long sleeves in the summer because all your outfits are short and see through.

Maybe she loves her self-respect more than she loves grow men's attention.

Maybe.

Or maybe she tried dressing provocative once and a weak man got tempted and tried to take it.

Maybe she's Muslim.

Maybe that's why she doesn't run around the city naked.

This is for the “fat kid" who spends his whole gym class, still in his uniform, sitting on the bleachers.

Those that make fun of him don't know he has asthma, a bad heart, and juvenile diabetes.

Keep your head up

This is for the “weird girl” with freckles, braces, bowlegs, and glasses,

who gets picked on while on the school bus, in the lunchroom, and sits in the front row in all of her classes.

For the 14 year old twin brothers that share the same winter coat, book bag, and mattress.

Keep your head up.

I know life sometimes gets you frustrated and fed up.

You also deserve a slice of the American pie, but don’t wait for it to get sliced for you; continue to work hard, stay strong and “stack bread up.”

Disability will never stop you from being limitless.

Unfortunately, “niggers” do exist.

It’s my suggestion that you pay no attention to their immaturity or ignorance.

We all have our flaws, some lie behind walls, while some others are just a little more apparent.

Keep your head held high your prayers toward the sky,
no matter if your biggest bully is your classmate,
neighbor, or parent.

It's apparent that you're different,

but don't run from it. Embrace it.

When someone who looks like everyone else laughs at
you for being different,

realize that our differences are what make us
individuals.

Know that there is no originality in an imitation, so
those that do so are the ones that are basic.

And as for you, the ignorant bastards who throw
spitballs at recess and crack jokes in History classes,

you might be in school and those who don't know any
better might think you're cool,

but I'm here to tell you that your actions are truly
classless.

You couldn't walk a mile in their shoes, sing a note
from their "blues," or take what they take to their
mattress.

So the next time you point your fingers at others, look
down at the other 3 fingers pointing back at you.

Then ask yourself a question,

If making fun of others is what makes you feel happy,
then whose life is really depressing?

Player's Club

"Watch the way you play your cards when you have a Queen in your hand."

So you're a player? Interesting.

What team do you play for?

The team that, instead of chasing dreams, chases the faces and waists of the same whores?

Yeah, I've heard about y'all.

You pride yourself on having a variety.

If I were you, I would be more worried about how many other "players" are studying these same women's Gynecology.

These women you pride yourself on sleeping with:

They give it up for fun. They give it up for ones.

They give it up to you and everybody else.

So remind me again, what do you need "game" for?

You think you've got the game in your pocket, when really it's you that is the "game boy."

If I've got it all wrong, then please enlighten me again on what you stand to accomplish?

You applaud yourself for having random sex with girls that only see you as a sponsor.

You love the game, but it doesn't love you back.

So tell me why you're playing?

It's Monopoly.

You have the car, she wants a free ride, but you need to park-her brother.

I'm just saying.

I'm saying, the reputation you carry should not be predicated on sleeping with whores.

If I were you I would find the one woman who is worth sleeping with forever.

Please Note: Sleeping around on a good woman will have you sleeping on the floor.

If her thoughts about what you're doing behind her back makes her feel like she doesn't want to sleep with you,

you can only imagine how she feels about taking her clothes off and being a "freak" with you.

So I think it's time you reconsider living out that "How to be a Player" stuff.

Before you turn around and you're in your 40s now, your "Black Book" has turned brown,

and the few hairs you have left are turning gray and stuff.

Before you start jumping to conclusions,

This isn't a message from a player hater, just a former player who decided to take on coaching.

So since this message has reached you,

allow this message to teach you.

Keeping one woman consistently happy should be your main focus.

Now that's a real player.

Playing your part in keeping your woman in her rightful position, above all the rest of them.

Your gratification should come from a woman wanting to marry you.

Not another notch in your belt from having sex with them.

February 15th

"If you're fortunate enough to have love 365 days out of a year, take advantage of all of them."

Yesterday was Valentine's Day, but...

Don't get caught up on the gifts and "shit."

Flowers, cards, candy, expensive dinners and trips and "shit."

Especially if they were only bought to help you forget the SHIT.

Valentine's Day is nothing, if the other 364 you're ready to walk away.

Don't wait until you get some new shoes before you decide to leave. Start today.

On February 15th, it's all over.

If you think I'm lying, watch it go back to the usual.

If he bought you a new dress just to watch you take it off, then you've already lost.

Baby girl, he's using you.

My Brother: Yesterday wasn't enough. Make it last forever.

Together. No matter the weather.

Anything can be done once. What separates boys from men is consistency.

If you make today the first of 365 days of love,

you'll notice that she won't care about yesterday next year because you show your love for her continuously.

Her girlfriend's favorite lines should be, "He did what? OMG, and Are you kidding me?"

And she'll say, "Yes girl, he's the best girl!"

Fellas, your woman's biggest concern should be how she can compete with the love you give to her,

not worrying about if you're still giving it to your ex-girl.

Yesterday was cool, but tomorrow should be a continuation.

If you continue to do all the things that she enjoys,

I guarantee you'll enjoy your relationship situation.

Ladies, don't let yesterday be the band-aid on the bullet wounds for all the holes they put in your heart.

Let yesterday be the beginning of the healing process.

Truthfully speaking, Valentine's Day is probably the best day to start.

But this time, focus on the self-love.

I mean, you can do badly all by yourself. You can buy bags all by yourself.

The problem with most people is they take the term "settling down" to literally,

when you should really be settling up.

Ever since sex got easier, love got harder to find. Back in the day, they used to wait until they were married to have sex. These days sex happens on the first date, the first time they're alone, or the first time someone seems to be just a little bit different from the people in their past. This has caused a decline in the amount of Romance in relationship. Some women require less, so men assume they have to do less. To restore these qualities, we must put more effort into pleasing women outside of the bedroom. As women, you must be vocal about the things that you enjoy. A man can't make you smile if you don't tell him how. Let's bring back the Romance into our relationships. Let's bring back the type of love that isn't predicated on sex and intimacy. I guarantee you that some of us will have a new definition of what love is.

-Mike the Poet

Emancipation Proclamation

"All of us aren't as free as we think we are."

From Chains and Whips to Chains and Whips.

2 Chains, 2 Whips.

How far have we really come from the day we came off that ship?

From 3/5th's in the Constitution to being a "whole nigga."

They used to have to hang us from trees, you know. Now we're doing the dirty work ourselves.

Pulling our own triggers.

Go figure.

They shot Martin, they shot Malcolm, but Biggie and Pac's blood is on our hands.

They said, "We can't keep killing the strong ones like we used to and get away with it."

Then, they framed us but we didn't get the picture, we just enjoyed the picture of the gun in being in our hands.

They used to rape our women, and then make them raise the children like they were our own.

So I'm guessing that's why we think it's cool now for our mothers to raise our children all alone.

They used to pack us into plantations.

now we've graduated to the projects.

If that's the government's idea of a hand out,

then fuck their 40 acres and mule.

All that's needed is a dollar and Martin's dream for anyone to achieve progress.

They used to use the slaves that were too broken to fight back to tame the rebels and called it "seasoning."

Now they take broke rappers and give them a deal, some whips and chains,

but seeing them in all that ice blinds us from understating the similarities of that reasoning.

They told us that we were free to go, took the chains off, but we never left.

Maybe that's why we never left the projects either; the cheaper the rent, the more drugs and alcohol we can by with our check.

“Since I have to be here, let me take something that makes me feel like I'm not here, even when I am here. “

They put crack in our community because where there's a crack, there's no solid foundation.

Either sell it or smoke it, either way we've got you.

What you do with that metal spoon is the fork in the road between addiction and incarceration.

What they did to us set the table for what we now do to our own.

We chain our women with the fear of getting their ass whipped if they ever decide to be strong enough to leave us alone.

We're living a false reality; we judge our success by how many diamonds we have in our chains and the year of the whips.

But these diamonds were delivered to you courtesy of your cousin who this year is back home, still in 2 chains and getting whipped.

What do you think he would do if he had the opportunity to take off the chains and get on that ship?

2 chains 2 whips

New chains, New Whips

How far have we really come from the day we came off that ship?

Toothbrush

"Sometimes it takes a misunderstanding for you to truly understand where you stand with a person."

Did she just leave her toothbrush?

This is big.

This is really big

And it's sitting next to mine?

What is she trying to say? I hope it's not what I think. I'm not ready for all of that.

I mean am I?

I mean I like her and everything but we were just supposed to be "friends".

This means I'm going to have to put a lock on my phone, redo all my passwords, and I'm going to have to start changing my sheets more often.

What did I get myself into?

But I have to do it. Because I know she's going to start being nosey now.

After the toothbrush, what's next? Her comb? A change of clothes? Her charger? I don't have room for all that stuff.

This is crazy, I didn't sign up for all this. This is too much responsibility. Who told her she could leave her toothbrush over here anyway?

Women, always thinking they're running something. That damn Beyoncé.

Now I'm going to have to change all the girls I talk to names in my phonebook to guy names, have two stashes of condoms, and start sending Good Morning texts. Girls like Good Morning texts.

Wait, what am I thinking? Man, screw this. I'm about to call her! We're going to settle this right now. You're not going to leave stuff at my house without asking me first. Who does she think she is?

Him: Hello?

Her: Hey what's up?

Him: Hey, what are you doing?

Her: On my way to Church.

Him: Oh ok, we'll I just woke up. I'm about to go brush my teeth and wash my face.

Her: Yeah you need to; I got you a new toothbrush too by the way. I put it next to your old one. The 2 pack was on sale so I figured you could use it.

Him: Oh ok. Thanks. Where's yours?

Her: Um, I took it with me crazy. We're just friends. But I'm going to call you back I'm "on the phone with my mom"

(Phone hangs up)

Him: I love her!

Sorry

"Don't accept sorry. It's contagious."

Sometimes "I'm sorry" isn't good enough. Truthfully speaking, sorry is as sorry does.

If you keep saying sorry for doing the same things over and over, then I'm sorry, too.

I'm sorry that whatever you might think "is" will pretty soon be "was."

"I'm sorry" is never as important as the actions after the spoken words.

If you think you can keep coming back home because you're "sorry," I'm sorry, but you can be sorry from the curb.

Don't you know what sorry means?

It means, 'Second Opportunity to Re Ruin You'.

So if you screwed me over the first time, what do you really expect for me to do?

"I'm sorry" isn't good enough. When an older lady bumps me in the supermarket with her cart, she can be "sorry." When the delivery guy is late with my pizza and wings, he can be "sorry." However, when you lie to me, to my face, and you had every opportunity to keep it real with me but didn't, I don't care how sorry you are. You and your "sorry" have to go.

-Mike the Poet

Let Her Go

"If you're not holding her down, you're holding her up."

She's tired.

Tired of your immaturity...

Tired of your low self-esteem,

disguised behind high priced jewelry, expensive cars and designer denim.

Tired of you thinking that having a loyal woman, plus another one whose insecurity allows her to be a "side chick" makes you think that you are "winning."

I'm here to tell you that no matter how many high-fives you get from your homeboys—you my brother are still a loser.

Don't let loose women cause you to lose the respect of your woman.

I suggest you get your shit together before you lose her.

I mean, you have to work for everything else in your life, why when it comes to women should it be any different?

It's your job to prove to her that, by choosing you, she made the right decision.

Just because you ran across a few women who were too weak to demand respect from you, don't confuse that with a good woman who will accept that and nothing less from you.

The sad part is all she really wanted was

Respect & Loyalty. That's all anyone of them wants.

Without those two, she couldn't have cared less about all that extra shit.

She had every intention of riding for you,

but before you got under her, you couldn't even have the decency to make sure you were over your ex & shit.

If you can't give her what she needs,

let her go.

If you're unsure of what real women require, then it's my duty to let you know:

She needs a man.

That means she needs you to be her rock,

in a world full of "quick sand" love.

She's known to fall quick, but the men she's always fallen for were never as quick to stand up.

She needs you to change her idea of what she thought a "man" was.

She needs you to bring more to the table than just your penis and a fan club.

She needs you to be strong for her.

She needs you to be the guy that the girl sings about in her favorite love song for her.

If you can't handle at least these responsibilities then do the responsible thing and let her know that you're wrong for her.

"Sometimes they won't let you go though. Sometimes you've got to walk away on your own. Not because you want you, but because you have to. Because being alone is better than being a fool. The longer you tolerate one percent less than what you absolutely know you deserve, the longer they will think it's okay to short change you. You know what they say, "if you give a mouse some cheese, they will ask for a cracker."

-Mike the Poet

Cold World

"Cool isn't as cool as it used to be"

The things y'all call "cool" make me not want to be cool no more.

But it was my mistake by following y'all in the first place, but that's the end of that, I don't want to be a fool no more.

So it's cool to be in a relationship and still sleep with other people?

It's cool to disrespect our women, treat them like property when they're at least our equal?

It's cool to be a criminal?

It's cool to go to jail because making out of high school isn't cool enough, so you're really cool if you make it out of prison too?

It's cool to follow the crowd instead of being an individual?

It's cool to have a dinner date at Outback, while your kids are back home eating generic cereal?

It's cool to call yourself Muslim without having opened the Koran?

It's cool to spend the night at somebody else's house and leave your children with your mom?

It's cool to only vote for the President and ignore the race for Governor, Mayor, and State Rep?

It's cool to not pay all your bills before you run to the mall and spend half your paycheck?

It's cool to have sex without latex?

It's cool to make the person you're dating look like a fool because when someone who might look better than them asks you if you're seeing someone, something becomes hard, so it's becomes hard for you to say yes?

It's cool to be an asshole for no reason?

It's cool for your 9 year old daughter to have barrettes in her 6 inches of damaged natural hair but yours is 30 and Indonesian?

It's cool to think “quantity over quantity” so you run from being in a relationship?

It's cool to let your desire to be in a relationship make you settle for some basic shit?

It’s cool to miss child support payments but not miss an opportunity to impress some new chick?

It’s cool to take child support payments and use it as spending money” for you Memorial Day, Miami, or Cancun trip?

If that’s everybody’s idea of cool, then I’m cool, on being cool.

Maybe

"Sometimes the person with the problem is the problem."

They want to know what happened to the good guys.

What happened to the guys that want more from me than my body?

What happened to the guys that want me to be in their head as bad as they want me to be in their bed?

Well maybe the answer is you *bad bitches*.

Maybe the reason you can't find your Mr. Right is because you're not his queen, you're one of those:

"You ain't got to treat me right, just treat me to some new shoes and a few bags" bitches.

The Bad Bitch: killing a man's desire to be good, one free fuck at a time.

I'm not talking about the women that expect a man to provide for his woman, that's to be expected.

I'm talking about "you bitches" You:

"As long as you slide me a couple hundred, you can have your cake and eat it, too" bitches.

So when a real man just wants to penetrate your thoughts, you become "lost and don't know what to do" bitches.

Maybe it's your fault

Maybe you should stop putting all the good guys in the friend zone.

Maybe if you stop trying to fill your pockets instead of heart, you would start bringing a better quality of men home.

What women must understand is that a man doing something for you should be seen as appreciation of you, not expectation of getting something from you.

"I need somebody real, somebody who's not going to fold under the pressure. I need somebody who understands it's not about money, gifts or trips, but it's about effort. I'm at a point in my life where I don't need "friends with benefits," a "boo," or somebody to sleep with. I'm past that. I need a partner, somebody who wants to be here. Somebody who has my back. Somebody who will go to war with me. If that's not you, that's okay. Just don't waste my time. They're not making any more of that."

-Mike the Poet

Show Your Love

"Those who receive love must also give love."

If you know you've got a good man,

go out of your way to show him that you appreciate his presence.

That means doing more than giving him your "box," or giving him some meaningless mall purchases and other presents.

Men need affection, too.

Men are afraid of rejection, too.

Men also believe they are 'one of one' so they feel the need to feel that they are special, too.

Try this.

Try stroking his ego as well as you do his other parts.

Most women think the proof is in their pudding,

so they give away the milk, not knowing sex is not where the loving starts.

Before he conquers your insides, start with your heart.

The real warmth he needs from you is not found where he feeds from you.

His woman needs to be his healer;

some men need to hold hands when they get needles, too.

Needless to say, showing your appreciation to your man requires a "humble respect."

Humble enough to let him be your leader during the tough times,

Respect enough of what he does for you consistently, to spontaneously take him out for a change and pick up the check.

But also don't be afraid to check him when he doesn't meet your expectations.

Furthermore, understand that Rome wasn't built in a day, so even a good man will need your patience.

He may also need to be your patient. It's more than sexual healing though.

Appreciate his masculinity by all means, but don't forget that he has feelings though.

What he needs from you is understanding.

He needs you to understand that he's not perfect.

He needs you to understand that he may not be the richest man,

but nonetheless he treats you like a queen, and that alone is what makes him worth it.

Understand that he's not the one you left for him.

Understand that if you compare him to those you loved previously you will never see the best in him.

Invest in him.

Mentally. Physically. Emotionally.

Step your "woman" up; if he brings home the bacon, at least know what to do with the groceries.

Cook for him. Be a "good look" for him.

Let him know that you're by his side till the day you die and shots could even get took for him.

Show him that he didn't make a mistake by pursuing you.

Show him that your fit is like a glove.

Show him affection.

Show him aggression.

Show him nothing, but love.

Sex is Important

"To fully conquer a woman's heart, you must be able to satisfy her mentally AND physically."

Sometimes, you've just got to rip her clothes off and show her who the boss is.

If you can't "hit it right," then you might get left.

Then the whole thing could go terribly wrong.

Every woman needs to know she can be satisfied by the man she calls her own.

The reason why most people step outside is because someone isn't handling their business at home.

Any woman that says sex isn't important is a liar.

When she's burning up on the inside,

she's going to need you and your "hose" to put out that fire.

Sex might not be everything, but sometimes sex is the one thing that makes everything better.

You learn to appreciate snowstorms and rainy weekends more because

you know that because of them there's a chance you'll be a different type of *wetter*.

Make love to her mind first.

Follow that by making love to her body consistently.

Let her pray that you finish early once because after every climax it feels like she's ascended to Heaven.

Religiously.

Make love to her. Cuddle afterwards.

Just because you've won her over, that doesn't stop the pursuit of happiness.

Run after her.

Know the importance of lit candles and a hot bubble bath to be ran for her.

Be by the sink with a towel, lotion and her scarf, its stressful being a woman, so take your manly hands and rub the back of her.

Then take it to the mattress.

There's a certain amount of education involved in having exceptional sex.

Study her reactions. Obtain your Bachelors.

Sex education is the difference between just playing around and lovemaking.

If you make every time with her feel like her first time, your requests for seconds will never have you waiting.

Sometimes you might even have to make it nasty!

She's been cute all day. Time to get her a little dirty. Go more than the usual 30.

She's worthy.

Don't be afraid to try something different. 9 times out of 10, she just might be with it.

It's okay if, every so often you just "hit" it.

But sometimes you've got to make her remember why she chose you. Don't say nobody ever told you.

If you do it right, she isn't going to want to do a damn thing, but hold you.

Let the results of what you do with your erections erect for her a new definition of satisfaction.

So slippery that it's impossible to maintain traction. Multiple Climaxing.

Please her. Get down on both knees and feed from her.

If you do it the way you're supposed to, you should also be able to drink, too. Turn her water on.

Loose control while you control her waist, she'll lose the ability to be able to speak, move, and think, too.

She's always been a freak, but it lay dormant because past partners were immature with it.

Get behind it. Now keep going. Don't stop until you force her to forfeit. No bullshit.

3am isn't the only time hormones rage.

She is a monster any time of day in the bedroom; she's just waiting on you to open the cage.

Bag Lady

"Bag Lady, please don't hurt your back, carrying all those bags like that."

She's got a lot of baggage: hate, anger, fear, pain, trust—you name it, she's carrying it.

Now she needs somebody to help her unpack.

Her mama tells her she needs a man,

but a "man" is how she got her hands full with all this baggage in the first place.

So her reply is, "No disrespect mama, but fuck that."

So she walks and walks and walks.

Hands full, heart heavy, stomach stuffed from years of being fed life's bullshit.

The real pain is in her womb, of all places—from when that bastard didn't have the balls to take "no" for an answer.

So he took her pants down, spread her legs and penetrated her middle pocket with his pool stick.

He didn't break her though. God Bless her for that.

She picked up her panties, pride, couldn't help but cry, so she just dried her eyes and continued walking.

She's strong as hell.

Weaker women have been through less and couldn’t live with the stress, so they found their comfort in a coffin.

He thought he could break her. Nope. Not her.

Not the Bag Lady. All he did was give her another bag.

She said, "At least it doesn't hurt as much the second time." Maybe because the first time her innocence was stolen from her, it was by the man she called her "other dad."

He’s the one that gave the Bag Lady her first bag.

Some nights she scrubs herself so hard that she bleeds, trying to wash away the dirt from that day. Ever since her mother let her “other dad” give her that first bath.

Damn.

Her “other dad” was the man her mother brought home when mama couldn't get over daddy leaving.

Mama thought her daughter needed a father figure. When really just a little more mommy and daughter time was all that she needed.

She was the prey, he was the predator, but every night the prey prayed to God that he would make a way for the predator to leave her. He didn’t.

Then she prayed her cycle would stay on forever, because the only time he didn't touch her was when she was bleeding. It didn’t.

So she left. Packed her bags, not as many physical ones as the mental type.

She was angry with God, cursed Him even.

She asked Him why He took the gift that she planned on giving to the man who loved her enough to make her his wife.

She walked. 2 bags in one hand, 3 in the other.

The one that broke her back was the one when she went back home to tell her story.

She had plans to finally put her bags down, and was called a liar by her own mother.

She still can’t believe it.

Let go and let God, Bag Lady.

Let go or you’ll die, Bag Lady.

It’s okay, you can cry, Bag Lady.

If you feel like the world has left you alone, know that I’m by your side, Bag Lady.

My Bag Lady,

Please don’t hurt your back, carrying all those bags like that.

Sometimes you've got to let it out.

If you continue keeping it in, it’s going to keep eating you alive. Cry.

Let the tears roll, and let your fears follow.

You've got the weight of the world on your shoulders.

You don't need another tough pill to swallow.

Focus on tomorrow.

For it is more important than yesterday.

Let your strength be your shoulder to cry on. Let the first tear land where it may.

Wipe the rest away.

As long as you did your best today,

There’s really not much more you can ask for.

Your future is your platform for improvement.

What are you still attempting to change the past for?

Dear Mike, I'm going through a really bad breakup right now. I don't eat, sleep, or go outside anymore. I do pretty much nothing. I'm lucky if I get up out of bed some days. I feel like my heart has been ripped out of my chest and stomped on. I fell like I'll never find love. He was my best friend and pretty much my only friend. Just wondering when this pain will go away? Kind of feeling like my journey here on earth is kind of pointless now.

Look. Make no mistake about it. In love, ***you are going to get hurt.*** *You're going to love the wrong person, for the wrong reasons, all while feeling that the whole thing is going so right." Then, one day, it's going to be over. You're going to get your heart ripped out and stepped on.* ***It happens to the best of us.*** *You're going to cry, and cry, and cry. It's going to be a pain like you have never felt before in your entire life. You're really going to take it awfully. You won't eat, you won't sleep. You won't feel like doing anything but crying. But guess what? You're supposed to do all of that. Why?* ***Because you cared.*** *I'm going to be honest with you, you might feel this way now, get over it, and 6 months from now, you'll meet somebody new, and it might even happen again. You know why?* ***Because you're human.*** *You make mistakes. That's ok. Because they'll never stop making ice cream, they'll never stop singing sad songs, and tissues are only getting softer. So go ahead. Take the day. Take the week. Take all the time that you need* *to heal. Get a big blanket, some baggy clothes, and a couple of really sad movies and just do it.*

Cry your eyes out. Eat junk food. Call your friend that told you something like this was going to happen 3 months ago. Buy some stuff online. Put on some Adele and just sing till your throat hurts. Whatever. Just remember that tomorrow; ***you've got shit to do.*** *You have to get back to living your life. Why? Because you've got to act like it never happened.* ***That's your revenge.***

You have to make sure that when they see you out somewhere a month from now, that it looks like they did you a favor by breaking your heart, ***because they did.*** *They gave you the opportunity to start over. They gave you the opportunity to get it right. So starting over is what you must do, and you have to be around and outside for that day to happen. So yeah it sucks, but* ***EVERYBODY*** *gets caught in the rain. So if you don't have an umbrella, just act like you don't even need one. Good luck*

Beautiful

"She never found her own beauty because she was too busy trying to perfect theirs."

Hey you, are you under there somewhere? I'm trying to find you but,

I can't see past the glued on eyelashes and pounds of makeup.

I'm going to need for you to be who you were before you got all the attention you have now.

Love the person you see in the mirror, first thing in the morning when you wake up.

You get tattoos to cover your war scars.

You're rocking 30 inches of someone else's hair, sometimes to get it to fit perfectly you might even have to cut yours off.

False advertisement: Miraculous bra with a matching girdle.

A shot of "depo" to get you thicker in the hips, sacrificing your one shot at being fertile.

I wonder if you would recognize yourself once you stopped trying to be somebody else.

Especially when you are already beautiful, without any makeup, eyeliner, or ass shots.

Every bump and bruise on your frame is its own beauty mark.

Your flaws are what make you flawless. You have no bad spots. Don't ever let anybody tell you anything different.

Don't let society's miscalculations of what beautiful is prevent you from being a woman.

The first secret to true "BEaUty" is BEing yoU.

Leave your secrets between you and Victoria, it's never a secret if your attire is always see-through.

You're not your hair, whether it's Brazilian, Malaysian, Remi or a wrap.

Your beauty should make any man that crosses your path stand up tall not make you feel like you're only beautiful when you lie down on your back.

Back to the initial issue: How many tissues does it take to wipe off the make-up that you use as your defense from your "insecurity" missiles?

If you don't love yourself first thing in the morning, then baby girl I think you need some more sleep,

instead of more foundation, more mascara, longer extensions and lashes, or more bleach.

I'm not saying women who use these things aren't pretty,

nor am I saying don't wear make-up or a weave.

I'm just saying that these things are just accessories,

merely wants when you want a different look, but in no way, shape, or form are they needs.

The fact that you are beautiful without them is what I need you to believe.

Believe that you were beautiful before television and society tricked you into believing they know best what beauty looks like.

Weather you're light-skinned, dark-skinned or in between, let YOU be the determining factor of what looks right.

"Physical beauty can be bought and returned

What makes you truly beautiful is your character.

Being pretty might get you some pretty things,

But when a man meets a woman who was holding it down before he got there, he makes the real investment and marries her."

"You've got me confused if you think I'm going to settle for just anything. My idea of settling down isn't exchanging house keys; it's exchanging vows and wedding rings. So if you're here with me, just looking for another notch on your belt, you're better off taking your belt off and putting it around your neck. If you can't do RIGHT by me, rest assured, you will get LEFT. Come correctly or you won't be coming at all."

-Mike the Poet

Where's the Love?

"Wherever one man lacks, another man has an opportunity. You're never too hard to be soft."

What happened to the romance?

Not only have we become too cool for school, we've also forgotten how to open car doors, send flowers just because, give hugs, back rubs, and hold hands.

Don't just hold your pants.

The best part of sex sometimes is cuddling afterwards.

We're gladly on top of her when we are in her, but after she's done throwing it back; we roll over and turn our back to her. Not cool.

Be the match to her flower bomb. Ignite a fire inside her without going inside her.

Show her your love for her is real, even when the lights are on.

Make her want you so badly that more often than not she's the one to make the first move.

Make the every time she does it with you so remarkable she will forever forget the first dude. Make her thirst for you.

Turn the water on before you drink from her. Mind fuck her gray matter, before you dive into the pink of her.

Your actions are your reflections of what you think of her. Don't only love her when her weave's new,

love her even when she has her wings on because depending on the woman, 5 days out of the month her love bleeds through. Now that's real love.

Every embrace doesn't have to have your hands below her waist. It's called romance, not "cop a feel" love.

So stop making excuses. There is no such thing as, "I'm not the romantic type."

The longer it takes for you to discover your softer side, the longer it will take for you to find a wife. So find it in you somewhere to take the love you have for her to the next level.

The only bands that will make real women dance go on the finger next to the pinky, and they aren't paper, they're metal.

Kiss Her

"The appreciation a man has for his woman should be demonstrated everywhere. Not just...there."

Kiss her.

Kiss her forehead. It lets her know you're in love with her mind just as much as her body.

Kiss her cheek. If you do it right, she'll still feel it on her way to work tomorrow morning.

Kiss her ear. Let her know that everything she hears from you is backed up by your actions.

Kiss the back of her neck. It's always a good place to start when you want to end up someplace else.

Kiss her shoulders. The same ones you lean on when you're tired. Thank them for being strong enough to support you.

Kiss her back. Women carry so much. We don't think they do because they don't complain, but even the strongest woman deserves to be weak every now and then.

Kiss her breasts. Whether big or small, they are what make her a woman. The same breast that will one day feed your children.

Kiss them slowly. Kiss every inch. Lips on one, hand on the other. They're a set. Treat them as such.

When you're finished, don't move.

Kiss her heart, the same heart that skips a beat when she thinks you're in trouble. Softly. Leave your lips there until you feel her heart beating through the skin. If you're doing it right, by now it should be beating pretty fast.

Kiss her stomach. The same one that carries life and those butterflies she gets when she sees you. Start in between the space in her chest and go in a straight line down to her naval

Feel her jumping? Good. It's working.

Kiss her hips. Thank them for giving her that walk that you hate to see go, but love to watch leave.

Kiss her knees. No, we didn't miss anything; we're saving that for last. You're kissing her knees because she was on them earlier today, scrubbing the kitchen floor for you. Every hard worker deserves a reward.

Kiss her feet. The most humbling gesture a man can show. It is then she will believe you when you say she is your queen.

Then kiss down there, until she begs you to come up for air.

Kiss her.

She deserves it.

Mind over Matter

"The man that captures a woman's mind first has won the war for her heart before the battle for her body has even started."

Want to know a secret about women?

It isn't always about the intercourse.

What she really needs is her mind fucked.

Mental stimulation. Penetrate her inner thoughts.

That's the deeper of the two holes.

Remove the layers of frustration from past players, as effortlessly as you remove her clothes.

Stroke her ego as gently as you do her hair. Stand behind her aspiration with as much excitement as you do her backside when she takes it there.

Try some conversational foreplay. Love her with the lights on.

Use your verbs to admire her curves whether she's in sweatpants or she's got her favorite tights on.

Make her respect your mind as well as she does the rest of you. Give her the best of you. If she falls in love with your brain, she'll make sure you feel it throughout the rest of you.

It might be just sex to you, but a woman's body operates in 3 parts:

a beautiful mixture of mental, physical and spiritual.

So my brother, you're going to need more than just "sheet smarts." So be smart enough to know that you can't get too much past her.

When you properly open her mind, it sends chills up and down spines, those types of chills may open her other parts a little faster.

Penetration before conversation leads to disaster. It might have you praying for some assistance.

The most important portion of this whole equation isn't making her come, it's coming correctly and that's done with consistency.

So practice communication as often as you do procreation.

This plan of action is not designed for instant gratification, so it's a must that in addition you practice patience.

Anyone one can be the one that she's with.

Your goal should be being the one she thinks about.

Get inside her head before you get inside her bed.

Make her thirst for your words of encouragement.

Don't be the one that she drinks about.

Be Great.

"Focus on your Focus"

You've got to stop living for other people's approval.

Don't let someone who gave up on their dream a long time ago tell you that you and yours are delusional.

Some people just don't have it in them to be supportive.

It's so much easier to hate than give love.

So sometimes when you two are talking, it might seem like they're telling you what's wrong with you.

But what they're really doing is asking you to listen to them talk about what is not right with themselves.

Some people are just not driven to excel.

Life is a road trip. Be careful whose car you get into.

If they're drive isn't matching your drive the only place you might get driven is to hell.

Handshakes keep the enemy at a distance.

Hugs grant them access to your back to figure out where the knife will be positioned.

Fuck any and everybody that stands in the way of your greatness.

You want it? Take it!

Those with ambition will forever intimidate the basic.

Don't let someone who's been in the same position since you met them tell you how to advance.

Don't let someone who took the easy way out their whole life talk you out of taking a chance.

Don't let somebody who every time you turn around is trying to be like somebody else, be the one you talk to when you are not sure if you are happy with yourself

Don't let someone keep bringing up your past to prevent you from getting a head.

Don't let someone who never worked a hard day in their life tell you that you work too hard

Maybe they just don't want it as bad as you do. You can sleep when you're dead.

Don't take advice about love from somebody who never got love right in the first place.

Don't let anybody tell you that they love you yet, if they can't tell you your favorite color, movie and mothers birthday.

Don't sleep on people's motives.

Those that pretend to be your biggest supporter might just be doing so to pull the wool over your eyes.

Take a second and pull it together.

We have to stop giving people permission to voice their opinion and let it have so much pull and power over our lives.

If your success depends upon how other people feel about you and what you do, good luck.
They fired Oprah Winfrey from her job as an evening news reporter when she was 22. Her boss told her she was "un-fit for television". Michael Jordan was cut from his high school basketball team. Sidney Poitier was told he should be a dishwasher. Madonna got fired from Dunkin Doughnuts. It's not about what people see in you, it's about what you see in yourself! If nobody else believes in you, I believe in you! See you at the top!

-Mike the Poet

You've tried talking.

You've tried shutting up.

You've tried working harder.

You've tried giving it time.

You've tried praying.

You've tried being patient and waiting to see if they wake up one day and magically get it.

They didn't.

Maybe you should try leaving.

"Did it ever cross your mind that the reason why it hasn't worked is because it just wasn't supposed to? You can't fix what was meant to be broken."

-Mike the Poet

Word to the Wise

"Often, the greatest gifts you can give a woman aren't provided by purchases, but are expressed in actions."

Fellas, No matter how good it's going, don't ever forget
the small stuff:

Flowers, cards, cute texts and especially the "calling
just to call" stuff.

Sometimes, that's more important than the mall stuff.

She appreciates your generosity, but just out of
curiosity,

did it ever cross your mind, that sometimes, paying
attention might be more important than paying bills?
Possibly.

If you need me to go into detail: Encourage her
aspirations as effortlessly as you do her passion for
retail.

Show her that she means more to you than every other
female.

Notice that new thing she did to her hair.

Don't be in a rush to mess it all up just because you
feel like you want to "take it their".

True love is not found in the bedroom anyway sir, you
just make it there.

First you've got to find time to get up in the morning
to go to church with her.

A family that prays together stays together

You're not perfect; she won't be either—that means you've got to work with her.

Worship her

Keep all your promises.

Her last flavor of love left a bad taste in her mouth.

So watch out for her insecurities. Let her know what time it is, consistently.

So what time is it? Its time you start making time for your significant other.

Take the time to show her your appreciation for her being the perfect mixture of girlfriend, homie and lover.

I don't mean the time it takes to take her clothes off. I mean, movies, blankets and takeout on the couch until the both of you doze off.

You've got time for everything else, but her.

Unless, of course, it's time for you touch her.

If she feels like she has to catch up with you to spend time, she'll probably roll—

as soon as enough courage is mustered.

Bags are cool; you've still got to come home though.

"Playing house" is what we did in Elementary School.

Building a home is for the grown folk.

She's waiting.

Waiting for the day you realize it's actually cool to be faithful.

The day you become wise enough to know that her asking for more from you doesn't mean she's ungrateful.

It means she sees potential, but she knows it means nothing without action.

It means she's at a point in her life where she craves more than just a physical attraction.

It means that you better get it together, because if she has to get it together for you,

she won't be waiting for you anymore,

but your things will be waiting for you at the door.

AS A MAN, you must understand the difference between being FEARED and RESPECTED. RESPECT your woman enough to know that her FEARING you will get you left QUICK. It's hard enough for a woman already, to be beautiful in a world full of hate. Don't let FEAR make her feel uncomfortable at HOME. One day, she'll RESPECT herself enough to not live in FEAR anymore. Then, you will be INSECURE and ALONE.

-Mike the Poet

Cut the Music

"There was a day when all we had was our music; it was our survival means of survival, our voice. Now it's what's killing us."

So you love *bad bitches*? That's a fucking a problem.

It's even worse when you've got a laundry list of problems and somehow think that being a "bad bitch" is going to fucking solve them.

Why don't you love yourself enough to know that being a "bad bitch" is a liability?

You like to fuck and that's a fucking problem because sex without love is an exercise in futility.

So when you put these 2 problems together and get fucked because you're a "bad bitch,"

9 months later you might trade your Gucci in for Gerber and then you'll be the "baby bag bitch."

So if you're a bad bitch, put your hands up high, Now wave bye!

Take a second; I'm pretty sure, with just a little bit of effort, you could come up with some better terms to define yourself.

"Bad" girls need more attention.

No real man wants a "bitch" as a reflection of him.

Remind yourself. It's not about what they call you.

It's about what you answer to.

If you have to question why they confuse you with "some other bitch," then without a doubt the answer is you.

If they can't properly address you, how can you let them undress you? I'm not judging though.

I'm just providing some education to remind you that you are special.

So if you're sleeping with two different men, at the same damn time, with no worriers and no condom, at the same damn time.

Baby girl, this isn't what they meant when they told you to #TurnUp.

Now you're at the doctor's office, trying to explain the pain of being burnt up.

Silly rabbit, tricks are for kids. Maybe this is God's way of paying you back for all of the "tricking" you did.

Some folk have got to learn life the hard way. Not to mention, these are grown men that you're fucking with,

so if the doctor tells you you've got the gift that keeps on giving, then that's what you fucking get.

Any time that he's in you, and his words to make you go harder end in "....you fucking bitch,"

Sweetheart, that's probably somebody you shouldn't be fucking with.

Let alone "fucking" with.

No one ever told me, that when I chose to be "Pro-Choice" my choices would be chosen for me.

-Perry "Visionpoet" Divirgilio "Fairly Odd Parent"

...So I guess that's why its mommy's baby and daddy's maybe. Because MAYBE he might get to voice his opinion. Maybe. Or maybe she won't even take his feelings into consideration because she's one of those "independent women". So I guess she made the baby by herself then? So I guess sex does a body good but having a baby is bad for your health then. What if? So what if in the end the decision she made turned out to be right? It's about the process though. Why is just her decision? So I guess because he didn't put on the "glove" he lost his ability fight? Think about what he's going through. You can't have joint custody in the Uterus or Family Meetings in the Fallopian Tubes. So the only thing separating a man from his ultimate purpose in life of being a father... is you. Think about that the next time you say "it's my baby, so it's my decision." Just because it's in your stomach doesn't mean that you aren't the only one that has to live with it.

Million Miles

"The key to long distance love is doing the right thing, even when no one is looking."

Distance is a lot to deal with.

Especially on those hot summer evenings,

sometimes the weather doesn't even have to be an issue.

It could just be one of those nights when you just want somebody there to chill with.

It's hard to share a bedroom when you don't share the same city.

It's that unusually lonely Wednesday night, when it gets down to the nitty gritty.

Let's not forgot the part distance plays when it comes to trust issues.

It makes it harder for someone to ride with you,

if they can't just put a call in, when your body's calling, so y'all can get it all in.

When desires for intimacy get her private parts in sticky situations,

she only wants to get stuck with you.

But she can't.

A flight is a lot harder to navigate than a 20-minute trip with no red lights.

What good is having you in her head, if she can't wake up, make a phone call and have you in her bed?

She can't put the phone between her legs.

If you two are going to make it work,

she needs you to be the man you are in front of her even when she's not around.

He needs you not to go overboard when your girlfriend drags you out of the house for a night on the town.

Have Skype dates,

poke her on her Facebook; shout him out on your Instagram.

Prove to each other that the distance isn't as big as the vision you share together.

Write each other lover letters.

Until you both see the writing on the wall without the need of a MySpace.

Use all this new technology to your advantage.

See the same movie at the same time in different theaters.

FaceTime each other.

Long distance relationships are the reason your phone has a front facing camera

Make plans for long holiday weekends; make the time together make it all worth it.

Make it last, make it easy, make it beautiful

Make it work.

Distance is not for the fearful, faint of heart, insecure or weak. A long distance relationship is the hardest relationship you'll ever be involved in. The reason is most people enter into relationships because of their desire to not spend as much time alone. So when you do decide to choose someone to give all of your time, attention, and heart to, and they are not able to spend that quality time with you because of distance, it puts an immediate strain on the fabric of the relationship.

This means the two of you need to work just a little bit harder to remove that stress. How? - By making up for the physical distance with being there more mentally.

Call more. Text more. Send flowers. Send cards. Have Face time and Skype dates. Have a movie night. Go to church online together. Have a game night. Anything to get your mind off the fact that they are not physically there. It's a tough road. It's surely not for those who aren't strong enough to be alone. You must really ask yourself if you can handle it, because it's not for everybody

-Mike the Poet

Turn Up

"The greatest gift you can ever give yourself is long term financial independence. Money isn't everything, but it's the only thing everyone hates asking someone else for. "

"I bet you won't Turn Up!"

The pressure you put on yourself.

Stop eating off the plates of others and "get on" yourself.

You always want some help.

Well, guess what? "Gimme" got shot.

"Can I have" called a cab, "let me borrow" called in sick.

So you're going to need to come up with another plan.

When are you going to get your shit together?

More moves, less excuses.

If you thought that 8am Math class was bad,

those student loan repayments when you don't have a degree to show for them are going to be ruthless.

The revolution that is your self-improvement cannot be funded on an hourly wage of $16.50.

Do you have any rainy day money tucked away for when the plot thickens and things get sticky?

I'm not saying you've got to go back to school.

I'm just saying you need to start focusing on your future.

Instead of being "Future" and "looking for her." What good is finding her, if you're a loser?

What good is looking like a bag of money, if your bag doesn't have any money in it?

I'm glad you've moved out of your mama's house.

Now let's work on getting you one of your own.

You'll never own one as long as you're renting.

That goes for those cars, too.

What is good is driving a relevant vehicle, if you've got to take it back to Enterprise?

What you have on should never be worth more than you have in your account.

It's not an outfit then, but more like a disguise.

$600 for a belt, but no furniture? No sir, you're not hurting them. You're only hurting yourself.

You're not fly; you're living a lie—not a boss, just the help.

You should go work for those labels that you advertise. At least then you would get a discount.

15% off, to go with your 15 minutes of fame.

You wait in line overnight for sneakers;

I just need 5 minutes to give you game.

Gangsta.

"Been spendin' most their lives, livin' in the gangsta's paradise"

Damn it feels good to be Gangsta. Best job I ever had.

But I don't really have anything to compare it to, because I've been a Gangsta all my life.

Damn it feels good to be Gangsta. All the women love me and I love them all back.

Until you figured out they loved the money not you. The woman who tries to stop you from being a Gangsta is the one you want to make your wife.

Damn it feels good to be a Gangsta. I've been doing it for 2 years and my mom still hasn't found out.

That's until one of the other Gangstas finds out I keep all the drugs in my mom's house, and I walk in one day and see my mom knocked out.

Damn it feels good to be a Gangsta. No commute, no boss, and my offices are the corner and the curb.

Until I'm in front of the judge because of these drugs, and I wait for him to tell me how much time I've got to serve.

Damn it feels good to be a Gangsta. They pray for peace, I carry a piece.

Until I run across another Gangsta whose more Gangsta than me. Then I'll need 6 of my friends to carry me.

Damn it feels good to be a Gangsta. I made more money this week than some people make in a year.

But no matter how much money you get, you'll be nothing more than a Gangsta your whole career.

Damn it feels good to be a Gangsta. Everybody knows me in my hood.

Until you get knee deep into some Gangsta shit, those same neighbors are not going to have any problem turning you in, and deep down you know they would.

Damn it feels good to be a Gangsta. I learned from the Gangstas I watch on TV.

But those actors get paid millions of dollars to play a Gangsta in a movie, compared to them; you're being a Gangsta for damn near free.

Damn it feels good to be a Gangsta. I'm outside most days until I see the sun.

Until you and your Gangsta girlfriend have a little boy together, and he asks you,

Dad can I be one?

Will it still feel good to be a Gangsta?

Didn't think so.

Running Scared

"When you run from a problem, you also run from the solution."

Boy likes girl.

Girl is scared.

Because all that the last boy that girl liked took was advantage—whenever he wasn't trying to take it there.

So now new boy works twice as hard.

Girl that boy likes, likes boy, too, which makes the situation twice as odd.

The problem is, girl has already felt like this before.

2-hour phone conversations and all that cool shit before.

New boy is different, but old boy has girl on some "all these men are the same" tip.

Why is it that when a man finally realizes that you're a woman, and wants to treat you like one, he must be on some "game" tip?

So finally girls let boy in

Now boy notices that girl has a wall up.

Dear Girl: I see that you've got a wall up. Be mindful, not all boys are going to be interested in climbing over.

They may not necessarily be afraid of heights,

just worried that once they put in the effort, all they'll get in return is a cold shoulder.

It isn't the new guy's fault that you have that wall up, but all he's left with are leftovers.

Your ex picked what he wanted from you.

Never had plans of loving you.

Had you thinking your only position was under the covers, until he decided to make time to uncover you.

You thought you found the one, only to find out you were even more lost than you were before.

But the new guy rediscovered you.

Unfortunately, for him though, you're scared to love again.

An angel with clipped wings,

it's time you rise from the ash like the Phoenix you are and fly amongst the doves again.

Don't be afraid to love again.

Your fear should be not experiencing it at least twice before you die.

I can almost promise you that love will make you cry.

But I'm just as sure love also sends people your way to wipe away the tears from your eyes.

Love is like a gun;

when put into the wrong hands, it can hurt people.

It can also be your protection,

the best weapon against the worst people.

Love might have hurt you, but that doesn't mean love can't make you better.

The tears you shed for fake love have you all dried out.

Real love gets you wetter.

Move forward.

Don't run from the pain, run toward it.

Your heart is your biggest weapon, use it with discretion, but never forfeit.

The longer you run, the harder it will be for the things you want to catch up to you.

Wake Up

"See, what I mean about the music is, it's changed us."

Okay, let's get serious. A lot of the ways we think and act are nothing short of delirious.

Point blank period.

We started from the bottom, now we're up?

We're still stuck at the bottom, if every chance we get we're recklessly spending dollar after dollar.

You'll forever be in the back the more you front.

2 chains 4 women, huh? Tell me more about how you'd pick a fight with your spouse to creep out the house and sleep with more women

Huh? You've got to be kidding.

Sometimes, the men aren't the problem; it's crazier when this is the type of attitude I see young women living.

When she's bored she lets men slide, like free rides at the park. I bet your Grandmother didn't stay out after dark.

Not only was she sure that if she came home after the street lights her mother would wring her neck, she also had morals, discipline and respect.

Ask her what she did for a check.

I bet she'd slap the shit out of you.

These men may love you for what you do to them physically, but would your grandfather be proud of you?

My brothers, the goal should be to make your mother proud, not your homies.

Don't spend so much time with your homies that you always leave your girlfriend home and lonely.

We spend money to buy things we don't need to impress people who could care less

We give people multiple opportunities to give us their ass to kiss. When we really need to give it up.

We give shout outs on social networks, like somehow followers are a reflection of net worth.

But we don't network with those who are beneficial to us.

Can we please get back to the basics?

That doesn't mean being a basic chick and giving it to everyone that chases it. Or buying diamond bracelets.

They're still chains. Material shit is our new master. We're our own natural disaster. But we won't face it.

In this life, no one is going to give you a damn thing. If you want it bad enough, take it. Let YOU be the only factor in determining whether or not you make it. Those that weight for handouts usually only get handed out the leftovers.

-Mike Poet

Missing in Action

"The man who can walk the earth and not know on any given day the health, location, and status of his child, is the biggest coward of them all."

That little boy you neglect has your blood in him.

He's the next chapter in your legacy.

You don't claim him though.

Yet, you claim these girls that don't belong to you.

That's the cool thing to do now though,

allegedly.

Instead of assuming the position of his first role model, you've successfully created his first enemy.

But when you were offered the opportunity to be intimate with his mother, you had all kinds of energy?

Ain't nobody got time for that.

But apparently, it's pretty popular.

But your daughter is pretty too.

She needs her dad as bad as the girls you try to impress need those bags.

So what's stopping you?

Where are you Daddy? Your sons and daughters need you.

You weren't this hard to find when mom was taking her clothes off, trying to feed you.

Now you're harder to find than 17-year-old virgins.

Your daughter isn't one of them, no bird and bee convo from you—she got the clinic version.

She can sign the consent form for her abortion,

but no luck on buying the Newport's.

Drug dealing and stealing are your son's 2 favorite sports.

When they should be Love and Basketball.

Plus, he doesn't go to class at all.

What for? He has no dad that he's scared to come home and answer to.

So 10 years from when you question why they have so much hate in their heart towards their "father,"

look no further than the mirror because the answer's you.

Your daughter is going find it hard be able to love a man.

When the one man who was supposed to love her unconditionally never bothered to show up.

How can you sleep with yourself?

I pray you get a lifetime of morning sickness for every day of her pregnancy that you missed.

For every meal your kids miss, I hope you throw up.

Don't think that all of your family's problems are solved because you're on time with your child support check.

A check could never take the place of time because checks don't come with conversations about drugs, college, money, or sex.

So I need you to be the father that your father probably never was to you.

When you sacrifice the opportunity to be a father to be with other women,

the people who are really getting fucked are your children—not you.

Why you're Single

"Sometimes people need a reminder of why they are still running the race. Just because you can't see the finish line, doesn't mean you stop running. "

You're single because you didn't **settle**.

You're single because you **know your worth** and won't take anything less than what you deserve

You're single because you don't need to be with somebody to **validate** your existence.

You're single because you haven't met anybody **on your level.**

You're single because **being single is fun** too

You're single because before you decide to get in a relationship with somebody, you need to **see more** from them than material things.

You're single because **you have some growing up to do**, and the person that you are is not on the same level as the person you require.

You're single because being single and hoping to be in a relationship is way better than being in relationship and hoping one day to be single.

You're single because there is someone out there that is going to love you for you, **just the way you are**.

You're single because there is a **shortage** of people who actually understand and appreciate the idea of being in love, being faithful, and longevity.

You're single because it **isn't your time yet.**

You're single because you know the difference between potential and bull shit.

You're single because you realize that a relationship is a **friendship** that turns into something much more powerful.

You're single because being in a relationship means more to you than what they can do to you and for you. It's about what you two can do together.

You're single because **you can do badly all by yourself**.

You're single because you don't want to break up anymore.

You're single because **life doesn't revolve around being in relationship**, and you don't have the time trying to please somebody that isn't happy with them.

You're single because a lot of people have just lost their damn minds.

You're single because you want a **relationship**. Not another job, not another bill, not another child, pet, parent, security guard, user, abuser, not another Band-Aid for the bullet wound that is your heart.

You're single because being alone is better than being a fool.

You're single. And somebody is going to have to be **amazing** to change that. As they should be

Priorities

"Do you know when you go out too much? It's when you ask your child where they want to be and they pick somewhere else besides at home with you."

"Goddamn she's fine, but she parties all the time."

Now partying is fine, unless all that partying you're doing is the reason your kid is always at your mom's,

or at your sister's,

or with somebody random. Somebody who isn't family. Somebody who hasn't even given birth to a baby yet.

Yet, you allow them to be your baby's sitter.

Is partying that important that you leave your child with whoever wants to make $20 on a Friday night?

The craziest part is as soon as they make a mistake with trying to be the parent you should be,

all of a sudden you're "Mother of the Year"—scarf on, earrings out, wanting to fight.

You gave up the right to put your "freak'um dress" on every Friday and Saturday night when you took it off one night and created a baby.

You gave up "riding and around and gettin' it" to sit home on the weekends and allow your kids to drive you crazy.

Why is it that you constantly want to drive them to grandma's house, so you can party with your girlfriends?

If partying was that high on your list of priorities, you shouldn't have had a little girl then.

You're worried about where you're going for spring break but you never once stepped foot on a college campus.

You take five day getaways with four of your girlfriends, but come home and your three-year-old is still in pampers.

You spend 500 dollars a month for the maintenance of your fingers, toes, clothes and hair.

Why don't you take that money, stop taking your kids to your cousin's house in the morning, and take them around the corner to daycare?

I get that you're a single mother, so by no means am I saying you shouldn't treat yourself.

What I'm saying is that when you cheat your child out of what they need to get you the stuff you want, you're ultimately cheating yourself.

We all need help.

Before you're in a rush to establish yourself as socially elite, try establishing some priorities.

The gift of creating life was placed in your hands.

Your place now is at home being a parent not on the party scene.

I'm not saying you shouldn't shop at all, just sacrifice the couture for the clearance.

You must transition to investing in your children's future with as much excitement as you do your appearance.

It won't be easy, I can promise you,

but that doesn't mean it shouldn't be done though.

You've got to understand that you can no longer spend every single Friday night trying to chase the sun home.

Understand that you might not even make it out every time your childless girlfriends want you to.

Being a parent is about doing what's right for your kids, not doing what you want to do.

What We've Done

"If music and television are supposed to be entertainment and entertainment is supposed to be funny, why am I not laughing?"

Where is the rap song for the girl without a dad,

who didn't fall in love with the first man that took care of her?

For the single mom who made sure she was there for her son,

when the man who got her pregnant wasn't even there for her?

What about the reality television show that shows you what 16 and pregnant really looks like?

It looks like you're only going to be talked about if "beautiful" is what you like.

Where will the hope come from for those who don't want to sell themselves short by selling sex or rap music?

Where is the inspiration for those who don't want to sell drugs?

Hope for those trying to make it through the struggle of being the child of a crack user?

"Let's get these hoes on a Molly?"

How about we get these hoes to stop hoe'n.

How about we get them to respect themselves enough
to not show everything that's started growing.

No, I don't love them strippers. I love single mothers
on fixed incomes,

who make sure the kids have lunch for school everyday
and work doubles to be straight when the rent comes.

I don't have a stack for the freak show or feel the need
to be around popular people.

When you sell your soul to get your wrist cold, you're
bound to get it repo'd.

She's got that million dollar...

But you would have thought she was worth a billion
with the way she throws it.

Her body should have been tapped out.

Her girlfriend asked her about her body count and she
aint even know it.

That's why I don't believe her when she says she's in
love.

Every time I turn around her body is a party for the
new guy that she goes with.

Not goes with like grows with, I mean goes with like,
"don't question me, just go with the flow" with.

I mean, "I'll buy you some nice shit, so you won't feel
like a hoe" with.

She puts on her crooked smile to keep from crying.

He told her he loved her once; she cried oceans— not because she believed him,

but because she knew he was lying.

She was a born sinner looking for heaven.

She didn't know there were levels to being in love; she just saw a new Bugatti and started undressing.

Damn.

It's only entertainment. We as society have this fixation with the lyrics and lifestyles of Hip Hop. This fixation in some cases causes us to look too deeply into the lyrics. We see these artists and are fascinated by their lifestyle, demeanor, and attitude. We attempt to incorporate there lyrics and persona into our own lives. This is foolish. We must look at artists in the same respects as we look at our favorite cartoon character from child hood, our favorite superhero, and television show. Hip Hop is merely a source for entertainment and amusement. Otherwise our mind will have us attempting to emulate a life style we can't maintain and an attitude towards those around us that isn't practical for coexisting in modern society. We must realize that while the music may be necessary to offer excitement to its listeners, once the music stops, so should you

-Mike the Poet

1000 Words

"They say a picture is worth 1000 words, what are your pictures saying?"

So let me get this right,

there's this boy that you like,

but you're not sure if he likes you...

So you send him pictures of you in everything but a wedding dress but yet you expect him to "wife" you?

The pictures you send him have him only thinking about having sex with you in his dreams.

Then you're somehow surprised when all the work he wants to put in is in between...your legs.

Baby girl, where is your pride?

I pray to God it's under there somewhere.

When you find it, tell it to stop letting you post all of those damn pictures of you in nothing but your underwear.

If you can't,

then you also can't act all surprised when the first thing some of these guys that *like* you try to do when they see you in person is get under there?

Anything for a few extra *likes* I guess.

I guess the imprint you want to leave on the world is the print you see after you're done pulling up your tights I guess.

I'm not saying you can't show a little skin.

I'm just requesting that you show a little class in conjunction.

If all the pictures on your profile show your ass,

you can't be upset when they profile you, and your ass is the only thing that they're wanting.

Why don't you put the truth about you on your Instagram?

About how when you see yourself in the mirror after you take the picture, you don't think you're that beautiful.

About how your relationship isn't as real as you make it seem.

About how you know you're in love with a person that's really using you.

Yet, you wonder why you can't find a good man.

If every picture you take doesn't advertise what you look like after you've unzipped your jeans,

maybe Mr. Right would be in your bed at night, instead of in your dreams.

Dear Mike, What is love to you? How do you know it's not just the sex that makes you think that you're in love?

LOVE IS... Love is not about that 1 hour a day you MIGHT spend having sex. Love is about being happy as hell the other 23 hours. Love is waking up in the morning lying next to them. Love is watching them sleep and wondering if they are dreaming about you. Love is messing with them so they can wake up too, because it's a lot more fun when it's the both of you. Love is them on the toilet while you're in the shower. Love is going in the kitchen to make breakfast, even when you don't know how to cook. Sometimes it's just the thought that counts. Love is picking out each other's outfits. Love is leaving the phones in the house for day, just so you don't have any distractions from the outside world, just you two and love. Love is "let's sit somewhere and talk" and having a discussion about what we're doing right and what we need to work on. Love is going to the amusement park, waiting in line, sitting in the front seat of the biggest, fastest, scariest roller coaster in the place, and forgetting that you don't even ride roller coasters. Love is going to a restaurant and slipping the host a note saying, "it's his/her birthday. Love is paying when you normally don't. Love is turning the radio off in the car on the way home and talking about our future. Love is stopping at Target and getting some popcorn, gummy bears, and that movie you two wanted to see but never got around to it. Love is getting home from a long day, talking off all your clothes, running a hot bath, and just sitting there, until the water gets cold and your fingers get wrinkled. Love is drying each other off, putting on comfortable clothes and lying in bed. Love is about falling asleep in each other's arms. Love is not even noticing that you didn't have sex that night, because you made love all day long.

Friends with Benefits

"If you give them the dessert with the appetizer, what incentive do they have to stay for dinner?"

Friends with Benefits, is it really beneficial?

Is the same friend that you "let inside you" the one there to wipe away your tears with tissues?

Or are they the cause of all your issues?

We tend to not add tittles because we don't want to apply pressure to a "good thing."

The word "relationship" has lost a little value, while "friends with benefits" has become the new thing.

That's until you're out one day and see your friend giving those benefits to someone else—then you need your hood on when you walk past them and your strings pulled tightly.

You want to be angry, but you can't be.

A friend with benefits has no long-term commitment; your contract is renewed nightly

Your mouth says "just friends," but in your heart you see more.

So when the fact that you two are "just friends" blows up in your face, blame yourself not the C4.

You see, the more you closet your feelings for the fear of ruining a friendship or rejection, the fact that you kept your mouth closed will be used against you as weapon.

Closed mouths don't get fed. Close the chapter on the friendship. Create a love story instead.

You just wanted to be held tightly,

so you sacrificed your values for instant gratification.

Next time, just ask yourself, what's more important to you in the long run? Monogamy or penetration?

When you give away "rewards" without the completion of "chores," even grown men become spoiled.

How can you expect anyone to be loyal, when you don't require foundation before they plant their seed in your soil?

You allow it, and every time he goes inside you go insane.

You thought it would grow to be something more, but deep down you knew it couldn't.

So we're going to call what you're going through now "growing pains."

He goes days without calling, but when he does call, you answer on the first ring.

If a ring is what you expect from him eventually, demand consistency. That's the first thing.

The second is keeping your thing in your pants.

That goes for the both of you.

Make sure they are the closest thing to perfect before you let them close to you.

That's what you're supposed to do.

It may not be what your body says, but your heart will be extremely grateful.

Being friends with benefits has it benefits, but there is no requirement that you be faithful.

You're either single or you're not—none of that "in between" shit.

Either they want to be with you or they don't. None of that, "you know what I mean" shit.

You give them the perks without the position. What incentive do they have to work for you?

If all the work they put in is in the bedroom, then y'all two really have some work to do.

The cool kids call it "friends with benefits." I call it a liability.

They make time for you when it's convenient for them, and you're always just okay with it.

Stupidity.

If you'd rather not settle for a piece, then say peace. Don't be surprised when your heart is left in pieces.

Only one piece of you wins, by having a friend with benefits—the rest of you gets cheated.

Just Don't Lie to Me

"There are many things in a relationship that with time, energy, and effort can be fixed...Unfortunately a lie is not one of them."

Don't make me to "fall" for you, if you have no intention on catching me.

Don't promise me anything with your mouth that you can't back up with your heart.

Don't make me look stupid for believing in you.

Don't tell me what you want me to hear. Tell me the truth.

Don't tell me to trust you when you don't even trust yourself half the time.

Don't waste my time because you don't have anything better to do with yours.

Don’t try to impress me with material things, they are yours not mine.

Don’t spoil me with royalty. Spoil me with loyalty.

Just don't lie to me. Tell me the truth and let me make the decision.

We can work on flaws. We can't work on trust though. Once that's gone, so am I.

Don't sell me a dream.

I enjoy disappointments like college dropouts enjoy those Sallie Mae phone calls.

Be real with me.

Don't tell me you're here to stay "forever" if your idea of forever is until I decide to take my clothes off.

This is my heart we're talking about.

It will not be bought, bull shitted, or lied to.

If you can't bring more to this table than "just words" then I'll gladly direct you to the drive thru.

"I'm sorry" doesn't work for me.

If you want me, you'll have to work for me.

If this isn't going to work for you, I'm fine with that.

No one WANTS to be alone, but am I ok with it?

Perfectly!

You

"To eliminate the users from your life you must remove the 'u' first."

What are you doing?

It's seems like you've got a lot going on, with all that bullshit you put yourself through.

In the midst of saving the world today, don't forget to save yourself, too.

You constantly bend over backwards for people that continuously bite your back out.

You move backwards, after your back is healed. Then, for some reason, you're back friends again.

I'm surprised you haven't blacked out.

When things are good with them, their name is gold.

When they are in trouble, they're calling yours out.

Protect yourself at all times.

That's rule number one in everything, and I didn't have to learn that in boy scouts.

Don't let titles dictate a person's power over you. That goes for your friends, family your spouse, too.

Some fish to feed others, some teach fishing—I say, "Let them starve though."

Don't ever let anyone borrow anything you can afford to not have back.

I don't care if it's only until tomorrow.

The real question here is, when are you going to put you first?

When are you going to stop caring about fixing everyone else's problems before your own, and start fixing YOU first?

You give time, energy, love and money to people who leave YOU hurt.

When YOU are the only person YOU should be worrying about.

You are only one person; you can't save anyone, especially if they don't want to be saved.

If saving them leaves you in need of help, then who is really the one getting played?

"Everybody makes poor choices. Don't beat yourself up about that. Some people are great at pretending to be something that they're not. Sometimes it takes months, even years to really figure a person out. So don't blame yourself if it doesn't work out. Sometimes it's not supposed to. But once you know, you have to go. The longer you stay, the harder it is to walk away."

-Mike the Poet

One of One

"Not everyone will like you."

Your existence should not be defined by popularity and public opinion.

Don't let the opinion of others influence you, what you decide to do, or how you are living.

Be the best you possible

Overcome every obstacle.

Embrace fear with an "I am..." attitude, that's what makes the impossible possible.

It's impossible to be liked by all; some will hate you because of envy.

Don't let the negativity of one person prevent you from helping many.

Embrace hate and criticism, and use it as motivation.

Die for what you believe in.

Until then, kill them with dedication.

Be yourself. Everyone else is taken.

Take the time to discover yourself, instead of searching for ways to become popular.

Be Patient.

It's okay to just be you.

When you try to be what you see, the real around you will see that you're see through.

The copy is never as valuable as the original.

Imitation is the highest form of flattery, but the amount of effort required is minimal.

Dare to be dissimilar.

If you get caught up following the crowd, then you become the crowd's prisoner.

Create your own lane.

When forced to play by their rules, create your own game.

Assimilation is easy. Innovation requires creativity.

Harriet Tubman could have freed more slaves if they had only realized their captivity.

It's okay to not be perfect; our imperfections are what keep us moving in the right direction.

We are all missing something: money, opportunity, friends or affection.

All you can be is true to yourself and the best possible version of you.

To those who want more from you, give them your middle finger and the one next to it.

Chuck them the deuces. When you live your life to make others happy, you let two people down.

GIFTS

"The relationship between money and sex has become so intertwined that people actually think they go together."

Just because you do for her, doesn't mean she owes you.

A loyal girlfriend deserves ten times that much respect.

You call it playing your part,

thinking she's going to part her legs for a couple of outfits and a couple of trips.

If your idea of being a couple is sex and shopping, then I think you need to call it quits.

It's time for us as grown men to step our relationship game up.

Any *boy* that calls himself a *man*, but expects sexual favors because he spent a couple dollars is messing my name up.

Since when was the prerequisite for pleasure a couple of pointless purchases?

If she makes you pursue her first, she's worth it. If she does it for purses, congratulations—you've now become acquainted with what's worthless.

Bands don't make them all dance.

We run across an easy one, now we think we're God's gift to all women. Those who give their gifts up for free are more likely to be given the gift that keeps on giving.

You think you've got it good now because she gives it to you without you having to do for her.

But remember, every apple isn't worth eating, especially when the catering is courtesy of Lucifer.

You're just looking for some new grass so you can let your snake get its slither on.

Explain the logic in being proud you're the 1 she's cheating with and not the 1 she's cheating on?

Find a woman who does more for you than what is done when the lights are off.

Your standards and requirements should be more than how tight it feels and how it looks when her tights are off.

Whoever said, "pimping ain't easy" hasn't had the responsibility of being a man to a real woman, yet. Because the woman you really need to impress will sign her own checks, not leave you in debt.

So when you're out here "cutting checks", make sure you're checking credentials.

That's the difference between an investment property and a lease or a rental.

If you think she's going to go down and blow you because you gave her some money to blow, stand by to be blown away with a conversation informing you that you can go to Hell.

Power Circle

"Protect yourself at all times. Success breeds envy."

Friends: how many of us have them?

Not as many of us as we may think we do.

We think because they're always around when bottles get popped, that they'll be there when we get thirsty, too.

Good luck with that.

It's easy to have friends, when you've got money to burn.

If they magically appeared when the money did, those aren't friends, more like causes for concern.

Watch who you keep around.

Watch who you throw punches for and who you let throw punches for you, if it ever comes down to a fight.

Watch who you allow to have your back

because they could just be looking for the perfect place to bury a knife.

Just because they've been around forever doesn't necessarily mean they're honest and loyal.

Honestly, the ones who can hurt your growth the most are the ones that lie closest to you.

Your seed. Your soil.

When you fuck over the people that fuck with you, you're really just fucking yourself.

When you burn bridges for no apparent reason, it makes people disinterested in you, when you really need their help.

Show them what happens when they bite the hand that feeds them.

Don't let 'so called friends' bleed you.

The bigger the circle, the looser the bond—don't keep any more around you than you absolutely need to.

Watch who you call your friends; they shouldn't have the title if you don't have the trust.

Trust me; it will never work if your friends don't like each other. Unity is a must.

There are never sides in a circle,

just love for those you let in.

Best friends make the worst enemies; there's no way out once they are let in.

Rule #1: Loyalty over Royalty.

You can't buy friends, only "company."

So watch the company you keep.

Sides

"Options never become priorities when they were once okay with being an option. Want more? Demand more! From the Beginning."

Finally, you're in love!

You want to scream and shout at the top of your lungs.

Let the world know that the feelings you have make you fly higher than any type of drug.

But you can't,

because you're a "side chick."

A *Plan B* like the pill you're accustomed to taking the morning after you two take it there.

To make it fair, you're not in love if your love never makes it out of the bedroom, baby girl.

You just make it there.

Now that you've discovered the error in your ways, make it your purpose to be an entrée, not the appetizer or side order.

Don't let the repercussions of you being a "side chick" make you give birth to a "side daughter."

The daughter you give birth to deserves more than an explanation about how she was just a product of her father's detour on his way home to his wife.

Don't let chasing the ghost that is a man who doesn't belong to you let that haunt your son the rest of his life.

Your story is too sleazy for soap operas, but it's common and pretty popular.

VH1 will probably pick it up. I bet that will make you happy,

but not as happy as your child would be if she had a chance at knowing who her father was.

These are the days of our lives, I guess.

You were okay with being #2 as long as you got your hush money.

What's funny is that the more money you got, the harder it was for you to keep it from going public.

You want to let the world know you've got a good man, but he's not yours to have.

You're too beautiful to be treated so usual. You're worth more than an apartment across town, some shoes and bags.

What's good is being in love if you can't tell a soul?

Every Valentine's Day, Christmas Eve, and his birthday, your bed is empty and cold.

I know you need someone to hold, but what good is it if all they are doing is holding you up?

If your relationship can't be given a title, then please enlighten me as to why you are giving a "fuck"?

Allow me to let you in on a little secret:

You think you've got the upper hand because you're not the person he creeps on, but the one he creeps with? Think again.

His wife gets treated like Queen Victoria and you get 5 for $26.50 from Victoria's Secret.

Understand that you are royalty.

You're not an option, an alternative, a side bitch, nor will you settle for less.

Once you settle and become complacent and comfortable and the users have gotten what they want from you, you're less likely to be the next Mrs. Right; more than likely, you'll get left.

Dear Mike, What would your advice be to a woman who doesn't think she's pretty enough for the guy that she's dating? She knows he likes her, but sometimes she feels he doesn't think she's beautiful. *Well, I wonder if SHE knows she's beautiful. When she doesn't feel like wearing make-up to make up for her imperfections. When she doesn't have to use sex to display her affection. If they can't love you in between hair appointments or the day before a manicure, be woman enough to know that he's not the man that God has in store. Good Luck*

-Mike the Poet

Stay Together

"Relationships only work as much as the people in them."

Did you ever think that the reason you have so many problems in your relationship,

is because instead of fighting for what you've got, you find somebody new to replace them with?

Since it's just you and me here, come on, let's keep it real.

Everybody knows that when you're in a relationship, there's no such thing as:

"I should be able to go over a person of the opposite sex's house—who's not my boyfriend or girlfriend—because the text message said all we're going to do is chill."

If you wouldn't believe it if you heard it, don't except someone else to either.

The majority of relationship problems are really a bunch of basic shit.

Basically, just communicate, spend time and don't disrespect a good woman because you're too weak to say no to a basic chick.

Women must understand that a man's responsibility is to make sure his woman is provided with necessities.

That doesn't necessarily mean that when he asks you if you want a new pair of shoes, he needs to be introduced to who Giuseppe is.

Women need to know that a man's loyalty means more than any mall trip ever would.

You've got to understand that being in love brings more jealousy than money ever could.

Word to the wise:

Don't love the man with a $100,000 in his savings account who only gives you a couple hundred.

Love the man that will sacrifice his last $100 to make sure you've gotten everything you've wanted.

To the fellas: when you're looking for Mrs. Right, the criteria shouldn't be how fat her ass is.

The right woman is the one who's willing to bust her ass all day so you can finish up getting your Bachelor's.

If you think finding love is hard, trying staying in it.

Relationships are coupes with tinted windows, but nowadays, couples treat them like they're a tour bus.

The more you advertise to the public, don't be surprised when the whores start to show up.

Closure

"A broken heart doesn't have to stay broken. It all depends on what you do with the pieces."

A letter to the girl with the broken heart: I just want to tell you, "I'm sorry."

I'm sorry that the ones who came before me were bullshit.

From the "side bitches" that were never put in their places, and because of the look on their faces, or how they move their waists, they were made to think they were just as important.

I'm sorry for that rainy Friday morning he made your girlfriend go with you to get that abortion,

Knowing damn well you needed him—and to think, you were always there to support him.

I'm sorry he doesn't love you like he used to.

I'm sorry it took you seeing him with somebody else to realize he was using you.

I'm sorry about that time you went through his phone while he was asleep, and you realized you weren't as special as you thought you were.

I'm sorry that this happened 45 minutes after having sex and after tears fell from reading their texts, you had the courage to pick up the phone and talk to her.

I'm sorry you were just so sure it was love, but it turned out you were just another girl he was giving sex to.

I'm even sorrier that after all of that, you still answer when he calls—matter of fact; you let him fuck you occasionally, not because it's good, but because sometimes you need somebody to lie next to.

I'm sorry you did it again.

See what happens when the attraction is superficial.

Look at you now, can't go anywhere without your tissues.

Why? Because you let a nigga in that didn't belong there.

You know, they say, "In love and war, all is fair."

I say, "That's some bullshit."

They tell you they love you, but when it's time to show and prove, they're on some "play it cool" shit.

I'm sorry you didn't leave after the first time he beat you.

I'm sorry that, "Baby, I'm sorry" was enough for you to continue to allow him to mistreat you.

I'm sorry it's all you think about.

I'm sorry that "Fuck Love" is your new motto.

I'm sorry that now you look for answers at the bottom of champagne bottles. Pour it up, pour it up. Drink till you pass out.

I guess since you got fucked over, it's only right to get fucked up.

I'm sorry your dad left, or wasn't ever there in the first place.

I'm sorry for every teardrop that fell because you didn't even get a phone call on your birthday.

I'm sorry that his relationship with your mother didn't set the standard for how you should allow men to treat you.

I'm sorry if he wasn't there to teach you that it's about how they treat you, not how they freak you.

I'm sorry he couldn't school you on the difference between courting and extorting.

I'm sorry that your child's father isn't man enough to do the child support thing.

I'm sorry that you're reading this and reminiscing on the men that have failed you.

You carried crosses for these so called "bosses," and they turned around and nailed you.

Even though I didn't do anything, I want to tell you from the bottom of my heart, I'm sorry.

Because I know some apologies will never come. That doesn't mean they're not owed to you.

I couldn't help but notice your struggle, so I felt like this is what I was supposed to do.

Don't Fucking Touch Me

"I apologize to every woman who felt like less of a woman because a man decided to act like less of a man."

Too many women tolerate disrespect from complete strangers.

Shrugging their shoulders, dodging provocative phrases and below-the-waist gazes.

You make her not want to be beautiful.

Marking it off on her "typical nigga shit" checklist as "the usual."

She wore that dress because she was in love with the way it fit her. Not so it would draw more attention from you ignorant ass niggers.

It figures. You see a girl in short dress, shortly thereafter, you have visions of undressing her.

Matched with your short vocabulary, you use a disrespectful line when addressing her.

"Damn shorty, you look good as shit."

"Oh really? When's the last time you saw something beautiful come out of your asshole?"

This Asshole has a beautiful woman confused with a 'freak bitch,' 'Barbie wannabe' and a 'fast hoe.'

How the fuck does her wanting to show the world the gifts God gave her give you the right to try and take it?

I don't give a fuck if she's fully clothed or a shoestring-
pull away of a sunflower sundress from being naked.
Don't Fucking Touch Her.

I don't give a fuck if her shorts are more revealing than
most underwear. I don't care that you look so hard you
notice she isn't wearing anything under there.

That's her business, not yours—no matter what might
be going on under there.

Don't touch what doesn't belong to you. What the
fuck is wrong with you?

Don't blame it on the alcohol.

She would respect you more if your excuse were about
how your dad wasn't around at all.

If the Ciroc made you do it, walk backwards to
Manhattan and try pulling that shit on Puffy.

Give her a fucking compliment; you might even get
smile back and a "thank you" if you're lucky.

You get an attitude because she doesn't accept your
bullshit pick up line with gratitude.

See what a young boy, with a rapper for a role model,
without a dad will do?

The saddest part of this whole equation is the fact that
she isn't even mad at you.

When she said, "No thank you" and walked away, you
didn't call her a bitch. So for that you have
simultaneously earned her gratitude.

Jump, Jump

"Sometimes, the girl struggling with low self-esteem isn't always the one who doesn't take any pictures. Sometimes it's the girl who takes a million pictures and shares them with the world. She doses it so they can tell her she's beautiful because she doesn't think she is."

Remember Kris Kross?

20 years ago, they made it cool to be backwards.

Some of us are still stuck there.

Our children aren't passing their classes, but we're working on new stamps for our passport.

We pass port after port on 7 day cruises.

All to run away from a relationship that gives us physical, mental and emotional bruises.

Backwards, like running from your problems instead of showing your problems the exit.

Backwards, like fucking a person you like before you get to know them because you think that decreases your chances of getting rejected.

Backwards, like, "Maybe if I have his baby, then he'll love me enough to marry me."

Backwards, like, "I'm too pretty to work or go to school, so I'm going to bank on letting the way I look carry me."

Backwards, like robbing Peter to pay Paul.

Backwards because you could really afford to pay them both of if you didn't spend most of your paycheck at the mall.

Backwards, like calling out of work because the weather is nice.

Backwards because you won't call off from being on the scene so much, so you can work towards having a better life.

Backwards, like giving raw head, but won't have sex unless there's a condom.

Backwards, like helping your new girlfriend with her rent, but be on some bullshit with getting child support to your baby mama.

Your attitude is like, "Fuck it, she'll get it from my income tax."

Backwards, like cutting off perfectly nappy natural hair to make room the lace fronts, closures and tracks.

Backwards, like taking a vacation to come home with overdue bills inside your mailbox.

Backwards, like having your own man, own kids, own maxed out credit cards, but have yet to move into your own spot.

Backwards, like leaving the one who likes you to pursue the one that you like.

Backwards, like being content with being a "side chick" to a married man and believing that by being the alternative you will one day be at the alter as his wife.

Backwards like destroying a 3 year relationship for 30 minutes of sex with a stranger.

Backwards like fucking up your own shit when some else makes pisses you off and you don't know what to do with all the anger.

Backwards like sex before love.

Backwards like baby before degree.

If the only place you're going in life is backwards, then when you future shows up, where are you going with her or she?

If you put as much effort into your future as you put into find love, you'll fall in love with yourself so deeply that you'd have the patience to wait for the one that's been sent from above. Find other things to occupy your time until love shows up.

-Mike the Poet

Real Gone Wrong

"Real really isn't real anymore."

If all you want is a "real nigga," then you've already sold yourself short.

"Tell her what she's won, Johnny!"

Court dates, his other women laughing at her expense, all expense trips to impress you, but excuses when after all the screwing you did leaves you in need of support.

You say you want a "real nigga"—

Do you even know what real looks like?

You probably had one ride past you, but you never looked twice at him because he wasn't driving the type of wheels you like.

Don't confuse the nigga you think you want with the man that might be just right for you.

That's the difference between fighting for the nigga all the girls want and ending up with the man who fights for you.

If all you want is a "bad bitch," then you're in for the fight of your life.

I suggest you leave the bad bitches' for real niggas, and focus on finding your wife.

Be Better Than Bitter

"Never use your child as a pawn in the war between you and their father; once they are old enough to understand, they're old enough to hate you."

The plot thickens.

You found out your child's father has a new girlfriend, and sent him a text saying he can't see his son anymore?

Do you realize what you're doing?

A son without his father is on his own now, so he isn't a son anymore.

Congratulations! Now you've successfully created a bastard.

To a son, a full time father may be the difference between where your son is lying at the end of the summer:

in a college dorm room or a casket.

Put an end to all the back and forth and being petty—please get past it.

Be better than bitter, be the bigger person—if not for yourself, then for your son's sake.

You don't want the awakening of how much a boy needs his father to be at your son's wake.

In regard to your princess,

don't rob her of being daddy's little girl just because his love for you is only shown by cutting the rent check.

You don't know how many mothers out here struggling to keep the lights on would resent that?

He might have a new girlfriend, but his first love will always be his daughter.

Your compilation of greed and jealously makes you only allow his child support to support her.

If she can't be daddy's little girl, she'll probably grow up looking for love in other areas.

She might end up loving a guy who controls her, like you were supposed to let her father do, and that's even scarier.

Sons of a murdered father would kill to have their father back.

When your child grows up and realizes what you've done,

I'll have to write another poem about how he or she should get the relationship with their mama back!

Number 2

"The last thing a single mother needs is a man who makes it harder on her by doing more complaining than understanding. It will do you no good. If she even thinks about putting you before her kids, under no circumstances should you let her."

When you're dating a woman who has a baby, understand that they're a package deal.

Don't expect her to package her child up and ship her to grandma's house whenever you decide you want to "chill."

You've got to respect that, you wanting to get in between her will never come in between her and her responsibilities of being a parent.

Respect the fact that she can't bring just anybody home.

Don't try and wait till the kid is asleep to creep on over and make an appearance.

Don't even sign up if you can't handle the fact that you'll always be at best her second option.

What she needs from you is understanding.

Not somebody to help with grocery shopping and step-popping.

No, she doesn't want to find a baby sitter tonight.

No, she doesn't want to sacrifice the few hours a day she gets with the one person who loves her

unconditionally, to be with somebody who probably
isn't even thinking about making her his wife.

When she's free, she calls you.

When she puts her baby to sleep she calls you.

Respect her for being a damn good mother;

don't get frustrated because this isn't what they all do.

One man already ran because he couldn't handle the
pressure. Is the next one going to be you?

When you date a woman who has a child, understand
that the best you will ever be is

Number 2.

WHY? Why do you make her feel like she has to compete for you? Why isn't just her being there enough? Why does she also have to be a freak for you? Why is it okay for you to do what you want, but she must do what she is told? Why is it that when she even attempts to do to you what you do to her, the first thing you want to call her is a "hoe"? Why does trying to impress men that would kill to have a woman like yours make you down play the love you have for her? If this was your daughter that got treated the way you treat your woman, and she left, would you be mad at her?

Mike the Poet

Instructions

"I know that what happened in a woman's past had nothing to do with you, but you still need to be understanding of it if you're going to be her future."

She's got trust issues,

"I don't know if it's love or lust" issues.

That's why she's not so sure if she can fuck with you

or *fuck* with you.

Sex to some women isn't as easy as the rappers make it seem.

She has to make sure you have the potential for longevity, if it's going to be her legs she'll allow you to lie between.

Capture her heart first; a woman must be conquered from the inside out.

Pay more attention to her inner beauty before you attempt to eat her insides out.

Inside that solid frame lies a woman who is badly broken.

She was beaten, flew the straight and narrow, but was looking down the barrel of cheater.

She's just looking for her Superman.

Could it be you?

She'll be able to tell when you ask to know her secrets,

and not how she looks in Victoria's newest see-
through.

She needs someone who wants to save her.

Not a boy who flaunts bills and takes after Bill
Bellamy because he's figured out how to be a player.

The last guy's name was known by the neighbors

because she yelled it out when he beat her.

The man she needs now must know that he'll just be
cheating himself if he cheats on her.

She needs someone who makes her beautiful without
the makeup.

Someone who, before wanting to put a bun in her
oven, will support her in getting her cake up.

Her insecurities will have her prematurely anticipating
the break up.

She has a million men that would kill to lie with her,

be that one dying to be there when she wakes up.

It's up to you to break her cycle of depression and
disappointments.

Dismiss her doubts and disbeliefs.

Prove your presence is an anointment.

Disrespect is not an option.

Neither is her falling for you and you dropping.

She's fly all by her damn self; she just needs some company in the cockpit.

Disassemble the wall she put up.

The only time she should be in disbelief is in the sheets.

Distance yourself from any distractions.

Leave the trash in the streets.

She's not going to be around forever.

When you find a woman worth keeping, I suggest you keep her.

Keep her happy. Keep her out of harm's way.

The woman is the most delicate of all Earth's creatures.

A good woman is the total package, don't sacrifice that for a worn out box in pretty wrapping.

While you're playing with a box that doesn't belong to you, the one you already have will be home packing.

Pick Your Poison

"You can't expect to dance with the devil and not eventually end up in hell."

She runs around yelling on and on about how, "Niggas ain't shit!"

The problem is, she won't admit that it was the nigga in them in the first place that made him the nigga she picked.

She picked him because he was the one everyone else wanted.

That was just her first mistake.

Then, she picked the most provocative outfit in her closet to wear for him on their first date.

She picked him because of what he had, and that was mistake number two.

Don't pick a man because of what he has done for himself because that won't ever mean he will turn around and do the same thing for you.

Even if he gives you money, most times, he isn't paying you to stay; he's paying you to go.

So pay attention to not only who you pick, also think about why he picked you before you roll.

See what happens is, when the picking is based on all the chains and the whips,

you forget that the weak ones just use these things as tools to make up for the lack of character with which they're ill equipped.

Then, finally you come to your senses and you realize that he isn't shit,

but you don't leave because he gives you all of those nice things you want and you're a slave to the gifts.

You let him pick and choose when he wants to play with you, as long as he scratched every itch.

All while keeping you on a short leash, so it's no surprise that you smiled when he introduced you to the world as "his bitch."

Free yourself.

I believe in you. Even if, on most occasions, you don't believe in yourself.

What you need is some help.

Not the help of a man who expects you to get on your knees for his wealth.

God bless you.

Because the pressure has you not playing your cards, letting just anybody undress you.

I mean yeah, pressure does make diamond.

But not the pressure of feeling that you have to every man with some "cheese" to get the grinding.\

So the next time you're upset about how you're treated and you yell out, "Niggas ain't shit!"

Remember, you picked that nigga in the first place, so it's your fault, not the nigga's you picked.

"If you have a good man, and he hasn't done anything to make you think otherwise, don't let what the last one did to you make you stop loving. Maybe the reason that fell apart was because this was supposed to fall together."

-Mike the Poet

The Family that Prays

"Prayer changes things."

You can't rush love.

Don't let being lonely put you in position where the foundation is messed up.

Rome wasn't built in a day.

Build up enough potential before you open the bridge to your mind, heart, and especially your legs.

The new thing now is to wait 90 days.

Before you give the one gift you can't get back, try showing your love in 90 other ways.

The bedroom is the last place you should want to put the work in.

If you're working on ways to become one,

I recommend going to church then.

Three's company, too.

No matter how much you might want a person.

It's not going to work if God does not want them for you.

In fact, they might want you even more than you want them.

What you should want more is God to be in your corner if, eventually, you're going to sin.

The fact that you're lying down and sharing a mattress with them doesn't necessarily make them your partner.

Fear the man that wants you on your knees to please him,

but he won't kneel before God down at the altar. We will all falter.

So don't be surprised when you fall down. Just be mindful before you fall in love

because you can only serve one king, and it's not them as long as God is around.

Loving a person that doesn't love God is the definition of Bad Religion.

What makes it worse is when you know God isn't happy with what you're doing with life he gave you,

but you still don't change how you're living.

The family that prays together stays together.

The family that grows a relationship with God will grow old and gray together.

If you allowed yourself enough time to heal after a bad relationship, you would figure out that the reason why your heart keeps breaking is because you never waited for something better, just somebody new to replace them with

-Mike Poet

Second Chances

"Pressure makes people do a lot of things. Some good. Some bad. Every day is a new opportunity for a new beginning. The beautiful thing about life is that it gives you second chances."

This is for the girls who weren't ready yet.

For the ones who folded under the pressure of thinking that they had to please their crush.

For the girls that gave the one gift they can't get back because they thought it would be enough

to keep him.

For those girls who realized they were only really screwing themselves by freaking him.

For the girls who open their legs because head and hand jobs weren't good enough.

For those that had to ride him, because just riding for him wasn't good enough.

It was him that wasn't good enough.

Take back your virginity.

If he cares about you, he'll respect your "I'm not ready yet."

All erections aren't grounds for penetration,

some are just a clown's demonstration of masculinity.

For the girls that thought by making him cum, he would come home, but he never came.

For the girls who fell in love with a player, but weren't ready to play the game.

Take back your virginity.

For the girls who still live with regrets:

Never forget, but remember that life gives you second chances, so it's not about what happened but about what happens next.

Dear Mike, what happens when you just can't make a person happy? You try and try to do whatever you can, and they still are not happy, what do you do? *I need you to understand something. You are going to run across some people in your life that no matter how hard you try you will not be able to please them. You will give them all you have: blood, sweat, tears and years, and it still won't be enough. You won't give up though. You will still try and try and try. This is a mistake. It's a mistake because their battle is not with you, it's within them. As soon as you realize that, you will be at peace. You are fine just the way you are. Your life is meant to be lived. Not judged. Those that judge are the ones who hate because they are not comfortable enough with themselves to give love. Good Luck*

-Mike the Poet

When They Call

"It's 2am again. The phone rings. You look at the screen. It's them. Before you think about answering, hear me."

Wait! Before you pick up the phone, haven't you had enough yet?

Enough of all the excuses, the physical, mental, and emotional bruises—enough of all the dumb shit?

Haven't you had enough of all the "do what I say, but not what I do" shit?

Enough of the "worrying about somebody that doesn't give a fuck about you" shit?

I guess your heels can be high, just not your standards.

Why can't you fall in love with the type of man that your grandfather was to your grandma?

You really need to think about making that transition from boys to men.

As long as you keep losing your self-worth for the sake of "some boy" who knows how long it will take before you win.

Haven't you reached the end of the road, yet?

Aren't you tired of them seeking warmth in between your thighs, while your heart is always on some out in the cold shit?

Put the phone down and pick your pride up.

There's a difference between being with somebody that's “holding you down” and being "tied up."

Don't answer the contact stored in your phone as "Don't Answer."

What you need is the cure,

not another dose of the cancer.

But you answer anyway. They tell you they want to see you.

Your reply is, "any day."

I guess you'd rather take what you can get, instead of waiting for what you deserve.

Let’s not mince words. They want to get fucked, and you're content with being fucked over.

What's the difference between you and the women who sell it by the curb?

At least she knows not to get her hopes up.

Treat her like a Lady

"Let how you treat your woman be the platform for how you would want a man to treat your daughter."

What are you thinking?

You have a responsibility to treat her better than the rest of them.

That's more than just not having sex with them.

That means, no sneaking, no meeting—it's all cheating, even if you're just texting them.

Never give another female an opportunity to have something to hang over your woman.

If you are not done having fun in the streets, you should have never tried to establish a home with your woman.

A good man is one who does the right thing, even when no one is looking.

Fast girls are like fast food. Wait for home cooking.

As a man, you've got to understand that there's a pretty good chance she's been hurt before.

Probably a couple of times.

So forgive her if she isn't immediately impressed with a few nice dinners and a couple of lines.

She knows it's always good in the beginning.

So it's your job to prove to her that every princess deserves a happy ending.

The worst thing you can do to a woman is make her look like a fool for picking you.

Convincing her to stick by your side, while behind her back you look for something new to stick your stick into.

If she says she wants a man, do you know what the means?

It means she wants someone who won't go behind her back because some other girl wants him to go between.

Don’t let your fear of commitment make your woman find it elsewhere. If you play around in the street too long,

don’t be surprised if you go home and someone else is there.

Little Miss Perfect

"There's no future in fronting; once you've accepted what's wrong with you, no one can use it to their advantage."

You can't expect anyone to accept your flaws if you act like you don't have any. Shit, we've all got a few.

When they make it cool to sue for false advertisement,

the list is going to be full of girls with fat asses who don't know how to use them, the guys with clean cars and dirty apartments, and you

In fact,

if you would stop fronting, maybe you wouldn't be on your back so much.

In the back of cars, back of minds, you lay on your back so much I'm surprised you haven't fucked your backbone up.

You're only 25, with more miles than a '89 Honda, and the crazy part is, you haven't even gone anywhere!

There's not a single stamp on your passport.

The only ink you got was his name, probably on your chest, back of your ass, or some place else it wasn't supposed to be.

Fell in love with a G, so you tatted his name. What a shame.

You F'd with him, took E, then fell in love with the D, but now every time you C it, you get mad again.

You probably had to ask him for money, but sold a quarter of your self worth for a new purse?

Won't get a penny for your thoughts, but call yourself a dime, even though you don't have two nickels to rub together. What's the matter with you, honey?

When what you're running from is yourself, then obviously there are problems. How is trying so hard to be something else going to help you solve them?

Maybe if I put on all this makeup, then they'll notice me...

Ladies and gentlemen, there's no future in fronting. Leave the feenin' to the drug addicts and Jodeci.

Get your life back. Get your goal of being a man's most precious asset, best friend and wife back.

The decision you make now is proof that you're not living right. A man will only expect from you what you advertise.

Be as comfortable showing your insecurities as you are showing what sits over top of your heart and above your thighs.

That's the difference between being seen as a piece of ass or an asset.

If you make it known that your spine won't be conquered until your mind is, you won't be asked why you haven't given up any ass yet.

NAÏVE

"Don't let your heart trick your brain into thinking something is there when it's not."

Ladies and Gentleman, The word for today is Naive.

Naive is finding that one reason to stay with a person when you've got about 99 others telling you it's time to leave.

Naive.

It will have you making up excuses for someone that sound as ridiculous as the lies they told to cause them.

Naïve will have you thinking they're "just busy", "just sleeping" or just anything but "up to no good" every time it's late when you decide to call them.

It will have you thinking that the problem in your relationship is you and not them.

The problem with that way of thinking is, when you change yourself to please others, you change YOU, not them.

Naive.

It will make you second guess having strong feelings about a situation because they'll tell you you're "over reacting".

When this happens, the only thing that's "over" is the relationship.

But being that you're Naive you'll start apologizing instead of packing.

Naive.

It will have you using phrases like "maybe if I" and "at least".

But "maybe if I" will only fix half of the problem and "at least" means you're sacrificing what you know you really want and just settling for a piece.

Naive.

It will have you thinking that being a boyfriend or girlfriend, having a child, or a ring will make someone stay.

When the truth is, accepting the titles, responsibilities, or ring, is you accepting things the way that they are.

Believe me when I tell you, that way of thinking is not ok.

Letter from the Future

"I pray I reach her before he does."

I'm looking for her. So I can warn her before it's too late.

The pain of being a single parent is worse than any growing pain or toothache.

He called you baby, so you had his baby—but he wasn't even a man yet.

He jumped straight into creating a new life with you, when his life, he didn't even have it planned yet.

You let him "fuck with you", before you knew for sure if he hand plans to "fuck with you."

You thought that having his baby would be the glue to make sure he was stuck with you.

Now you're stuck on stupid.

If you think I'm lying, ask the 10.3 million single mothers in America, they'll prove it.

This is sex we're talking about; it was while since the last time you got worked out

So you got your Nike on and said, "Just do it."

You did it too well in fact.

Now you're waiting on a check from public assistance,

that's barely enough to support the both of you.

Having a dad around is a real child's support.

But you weren't his queen, just a member of his court, now you're in and out of court, too.

"I only knew her 2 months your honor,"

His only defense is that he questions the paternity.

And to think: You were one professional photo shoot away from ripping the runway.

Now you've traded your six-pack for some stretch marks, praying Victoria's Secret launches a line for maternity.

You spend most nights crying yourself to sleep because you didn't plan on it turning out like this.

You didn't think your life could change from you getting whatever you wanted to someone who's constantly taking food out of your mouth like this.

You love your child, but deep down you feel like you left a lot on the table.

Having a child is a gift you can't give back, nor is it exchangeable. You weren't ready or willing at all, just available and able.

He left 20 minutes after the sex was over, what made you think he was going to stick around for the entire pregnancy?

I hope this letter gets to you before he does. Before you think about letting just anybody stick it in you, remember me.

Love Doesn't Hurt

"If you have to ask yourself whether you should stay or go, honestly, you should've been left."

Teamwork makes the dream work.

If not, then best believe the two of you are in for some trouble.

The woman you chose to be your reflection should be under your umbrella of protection, not forced to defend her love for you through rumbles.

I understand the fact that you're supposed to fight for what you love,

but at the same time, don't let your weaknesses as a man make your woman put on her gloves.

There's nothing more heartbreaking than seeing a good woman who is scared to death of loving a man

because the only love she knew, told her he loved her after raising his voice or his hand.

Like, somehow, "I love you" said to her will make her not have to wear long sleeves to work tomorrow,

or, somehow, "Baby, I'm sorry" will heal that black eye before she sits next to her father at church tomorrow.

Do you know what a broken woman looks like?

one who has the definitions of *fear* and *love* wrong?

She heard once that, "all is fair in love and war," so she stayed, even after there was blood drawn.

She thinks *Love is Blind* is a love song.

Sometimes dark shades cover black eyes.

Sometimes the pain never goes away, years after the disaster called a "relationship," and you find yourself still trying to hold back lies.

To the woman who let one man make her not want love anymore,

I want you to know that all men don't love like that.

When they ask you to "fight for them,"

they don't mean for you to put on gloves, like that.

There's nothing scarier than a woman whose definitions of *love* and *fear* are confused.

One who cried her eyes out over the last one, so she has no tears left for a good dude.

When a good woman doesn't want to be a good woman anymore, the entire world loses.

Keep hope alive, because real love doesn't hurt, baby girl.

Don't take my word for it; you'll meet a man that's going to prove it!

"One of people's biggest misunderstandings in life is about love. Yes, love is a beautiful thing, but the most beautiful thing about love—true love—is that it comes with no outside obligations. Love is not a reason to tolerate disrespect. Love is not a reason to forgive someone who failed you. Love is not a reason to sacrifice your individual happiness for the sake of someone you don't even have to be with. Those are the things that make love so decent. When someone has no reason at all to treat you with respect, to be loyal to you, to put you before them, but they still do it, that's love. The longer you allow "love" to keep you with somebody that uses the fact that you love them as a reason to expect forgiveness from you; you have forgotten that true love wouldn't have even put you in the position to make that call in the first place. If you lost your job, love would get us through that, if you broke both your arms and legs, love would make me wash you up twice a day with a smile on my face. However, if you lie to me, steal from me, cheat on me, and I didn't do anything to deserve that, why should I respond with love, when clearly you didn't love me enough to not do that me?"

-Mike the Poet

Change Clothes

"For the woman who's tired of being a woman, tired of getting played so you want to be the player, this is for you."

Dear Miss Misunderstood.

Do you really think you've got the upper hand because you find them, fuck them and flee them first?

Sweetheart, I know your heart is broken, but your way of thinking couldn't be any worse.

"I think like a nigga, so I don't get played like a bitch," she said.

"If they can do it, why can't I? Their motto is 'fuck bitches, get money,' so fuck love, I just want to get rich," she said.

Since you want to switch roles, you might as well switch clothes.

Actually, it doesn't even matter what you're wearing or why you're sharing. A hoe is a hoe.

The only difference between you and a young girl, besides that fact that she doesn't know any better, is that sooner or later, she will realize the error in her ways, eventually.

As for you, you're still getting fucked even if you spread your legs consensually.

Let's think about this for a second: You "don't trust men," but you fuck men. Makes sense, right?

To me, it sounds like you've got it a little mixed up.

You're telling me that when they tell you how they feel,
you don't give damn, but when they want to know
what it feels like to be inside of you, you a give a fuck?

I think it's time you give it up effective immediately.
I'm not talking about your vagina though.

You're a woman participating in child's play; baby girl,
I think it's time to grow.

Grow to know that you will forever be defined by who
you are giving your sex to.

If you give it to individuals who haven't earned it yet,
how could it ever be considered special?

A key that opens any lock may be a master key, but a
lock that can be opened by any key is useless.

So with that being said, just because you're tired of
giving it to your ex dude, that doesn't mean you give it
to the next dude.

Make the appetite for your dessert require numerous
dinners. Hunger makes for the best food.

The number of men that have the pleasure of having
you should be only a fraction of those that inquire.

Before you hop into bed with a person, be certain that
you will wake up the next day inspired.

Instructions

"Sometimes a woman already knows her worth, others need to be told."

For those who don't know they don't have to settle for just anything, here it goes.

You won't ever really get paid until you know your worth.

FYI, the most valuable of items are never for sale.

Know God first.

If that's not love to you, then fall in love so deeply with yourself that only a man's voice could awaken you.

Play your cards right—don't let them 52 fake you.

You've been strong too long let these weak men break you.

You should be over dressed and over paid. Never overly dumb.

You've spent 51 weeks of the year trying to get over a man that gave you a good 1.

Doesn't sound like good math me.

Sounds like you need a "know your worth" class to me.

Well, lucky for you, class is in session.

Have enough class to not show your ass on social networks and via texting.

Leave the curiosity about how fat your cat is until about 10 minutes before you start sexing.

The movie won't be as good if you give it all up in the preview.

Don't let the fact that you think you need somebody be more important than finding somebody who needs you.

Be the woman a man requires,

not the "bitch a nigga needs."

Your most valuable asset is what's 18 inches below your head, not 18 above your knees.

Please, I'm warning you.

He might have gold all in his chain, and gold all in his watch,

but he put the gold on to see if you would be impressed to enough to take your clothes off.

If you don't believe me, just watch.

Just watch out for those who care more about how you look than what you're saying.

Actions only speak louder than words, if the actions are consistent with what they're saying.

Why I Write

So they're saying, "I've got next."

The next question is what am I going to do it with it?

Either I'm going to be the next one telling women to keep their clothes on,

or the next one trying to use my popularity as an opportunity to sleep with new women.

I'm taking all bets.

You see, popularity is pressure and pressure bursts pipes.

I just want to be next, to tell young girls not to let pressure make them a mother before love makes them a wife.

These young girls are scraping up their knees for these street niggas with no degrees.

I've got next to tell them:

"I know you're turned on by the fact that he's in the trap, but I need you to realize that makes him the cheese."

I've got next to tell young boys that there are ways out of the hood other than bricks and basketballs.

Fucking with these streets, your last brick won't move because it's going to be on top of the dirt where your casket falls.

A moment of silence for somebody you lost.

Tears come to my eyes every time I turn the news on.

What could have been the next Malcolm X got shot last night because he had "them foams" and some Tru's on.

2 Chains! They ask me what I do and who I do it for.

I got next for the girl who doesn't go to class at all

because she's busy being a "down ass bitch," to her hustler boyfriend,

or she's trading her boyfriend jeans in for boy shorts because the boy she likes is nice at basketball.

She's 16. Daddy is doing life, so he can't school her on how to get her head right.

Her 19-year-old boyfriend won't make sure she gets to school in the morning, but has no problem schooling her on how to give head right.

Shit is sad, right?

The only show she watches is Basketball Wives, so she starves herself and gets butt shots because all they talk about is having big asses and small thighs.

So, since I've got next, I'm next in line to play Martin,

not Payne, but Luther King, Jr. until shots from haters put in me in coffin.

I'd rather be put in a coffin for being like Martin, instead of coughin' from a loud pack.

Since I've got next, my next stop is BET, so I can tell them to bring "A Different World" back.

I just want my girls back,

before bands made them dance and everybody got turned up.

Now money makes them cum and cumming makes them come to the clinic often because turning up got them burnt up.

Since I've got next, I'm next to remind y'all that it's either condoms or caskets.

There isn't a cure for AIDS, unless you believe in Magic.

You and I don't have Magic Johnson's connections.

So I've got next to tell you that when you use your Johnson, it must be used in conjunction with protection.

Pretty girls have AIDS, too. Cute guys have AIDS, too.

I've got next to remind women that no matter how big your ass is, your brain is your biggest asset.

Next to tell young girls, "don't feel pressured because your girlfriends are wild and you ain't give up no ass yet."

I've got next so I can make an effort to get more brothers out of the state prison and into state college..

I'll do it by telling them that money, power and respect don't mean shit without the knowledge.

Thank you for letting me have next, my Instagram is @justmike_ if you don't already follow. Thank you for purchasing Just Words, I hope it was worth every dollar.

Dear Mike, I finally met someone new. I'm so excited. It's like he's the answer to my prayers. He is so sweet. We have been dating for a couple months now and he asked me to be his girlfriend. I don't know if I am ready though. My last boyfriend was like this in the beginning. How do I know it won't happen again? I'm ready to love again but I'm not ready to be hurt by love again. What if it doesn't work?

What if heaven was a lie? What if after you die there is nothing but darkness? What if the lottery is just a big scheme to get people to spend money they don't have, chasing a dream? Baby girl, life is about chances. Life is about looking the one thing you are the most scared right in the face saying, "Excuse me, you're in my way."

Could you get hurt again? Yes. Could you put your all into something just for it to blow up in your face? Yup. But does that mean you shouldn't take the chance? Hell No!

Why? Because on the other side of that phone, the other side of that bed, could be the one person who is the reason why it never worked with anybody else.

You will never know until you take the chance. I don't know about you, but I'm not a quitter. Why? Because when it's real, love is the one thing that can make everything in life better. It's heaven on earth. It's hitting the lottery every day.

That's why you take the chance. You have to play to win.

Take a leap, or you'll never know.

Thank you!

To EVERYBODY! Everyone who bought a book, reposted a poem, shouted me out on a social network, came to a show, and stayed all the way to the end to watch me perform. Thank you to everybody that emailed me, and wrote in the "Dear Mike" section of my site. Thank you for trusting me with your most personal of issues. Thank you for taking the time out of your day to write me, just to say thank you. You inspire me to put in long hours and sleepless nights; because I know there is so much work to do to help us get back on track.

Thank you to everybody that stopped me in the mall, the supermarket, after a show and hugged me. The love I get from you guys is nothing short of amazing.

I truly cannot take the credit for all the success I have. WE DID THAT. Every time somebody tells me I saved them, WE DID THAT. I am nothing without all of you. Thank you.

A special thank you to God, my family, my friends, everybody who gave me the inspiration to give you "Just Words". It is truly an honor and a privilege that you allowed me to assist you in your journey. See you soon

-Just Mike

Dear Trayvon,

I'm sorry. I'm sorry that the "neighborhood watch" that was supposed to be there to "watch" you, thought that because you had a hoodie on you were a criminal, so he got in his vehicle and followed you. I'm sorry that he ignored the police, got out his vehicle and felt it necessary to approach you. I'm sorry that they labeled you a thug because you fought back, I mean what the hell where you supposed to do? I could only imagine what it felt like; it probably scared the "17 year old" right out of you. I'm sorry that a blow to his face caused him to reach for his waist and proceed to blow the soul right out of you. I'm sorry that your friend couldn't keep it together during her testimony. I'm sorry that his defense was that he was in fear for his life, I wasn't even there and I don't eat pork, but I know that , that ladies and gentleman is bologna. I'm sorry that you're not spending this summer getting ready to go to college, because someone decided to take the law into their own hands and combat your innocence with violence. I'm sorry that you had a side to this story, but you died, so we never heard it. I'm sorry that your parents lost the only child they had together and all they got in return is a Not Guilty verdict.

I'm sorry for Trayvon Martin, and all the other Trayvon's in every community. It's not about race, it's about rights, your death wasn't in vein, praise the Lord, because it sparked a change in many communities. So I hope that you sleep well, and I pray that one day your mother and father will too. I could have been Trayvon Martin, so he took a piece of me when he took you.

Welcome to America, where apparently you can be the killer, and the victim.

May your soul rest in peace.

Amen.